May Alden Ward

Old Colony Days

May Alden Ward

Old Colony Days

ISBN/EAN: 9783742810120

Manufactured in Europe, USA, Canada, Australia, Japa

Cover: Foto ©ninafisch / pixelio.de

Manufactured and distributed by brebook publishing software (www.brebook.com)

May Alden Ward

Old Colony Days

OLD COLONY DAYS

BY

MAY ALD...

"...DANTE..." ETC.

Copyright, 1896,
By ROBERTS BROTHERS.

University Press:
JOHN WILSON AND SON, CAMBRIDGE, U.S.A.

CONTENTS.

	PAGE
THE FATHER OF AMERICAN HISTORY	9
THE EARLY AUTOCRAT OF NEW ENGLAND	89
AN OLD-TIME MAGISTRATE	129
SOME DELUSIONS OF OUR FOREFATHERS	187
A GROUP OF PURITAN POETS	235
INDEX	277

THE
FATHER OF AMERICAN HISTORY.

OLD COLONY DAYS.

THE FATHER OF AMERICAN HISTORY.

BROWNING has tried to show us that it is better to live poetry than to write it, although he could do both. For different reasons it is a grander thing to make history than to be merely the recorders of it. But when the makers of noble history are also its writers, then is the world fortunate.

As Americans we can never be grateful enough that in the little band of men who first set foot on Plymouth Rock was one who realized that they were making history, one who felt that that rock was to become the corner-stone of a nation. He saw that from the moment when they first resolved for freedom's sake "to tempt the dangers of an unknown sea, to plant a home in an unknown wilderness," their lightest acts became important and worthy of recording. To him we owe the chart by which we follow this heroic band step by step, day after day, through the long privations, the terrible sufferings, and the crushing sorrows which attended the birth of New England.

Now that Forefathers' Day is celebrated from the Atlantic to the Pacific, and a splendid monument marks the scene of their martyrdom; now that great paintings of the embarkation and of the landing adorn not only the walls of Pilgrim Hall at Plymouth, but the Rotunda of the Capitol at Washington, and the Peers' Corridor of the House of Parliament, — we are apt to forget what very unimportant events these were at the time of their occurrence. We cannot realize how little noise they made in the world, and how easily all record of them might have been lost. England took no note either of the embarkation or of the landing; and the Peers would have been mightily amused had it been suggested to them that the departure of that little band of stubborn "Separatists" was an event of historical importance, worthy to be perpetuated on the walls of the House of Parliament. Painters, poets, and historians would have been dependent on imagination and tradition in portraying these scenes were it not for the pen of William Bradford, to whom belongs, unquestionably, the title of "The Father of American History."

By this opinion no slight is intended to his famous contemporaries. Their greatness lay chiefly in other directions. Some touches, it is true, were added to the history by Edward Winslow; but his sketches, rare treasures as they are, narrate only detached incidents. To Bradford alone belongs the credit of having written a connected history of the "Old

Colony" during the first quarter century of its existence, while it was still doubtful whether it was to exist at all. He must be placed first in that great triumvirate of Plymouth men of whom it has been said that Standish was the hand, Winslow the tongue, and Bradford the guiding brain.

Volumes upon volumes have been written since; but whoever would live again the life of the Pilgrims and feel their very presence, must go back to three old books, "Mourt's Relation," "Bradford's Letter Book," and "Bradford's History," written more than two centuries and a half ago. Each of these works had curious adventures of its own before it reached us in its present permanent form. The quaint little book called "Mourt's Relation" contains Bradford's journal during that first eventful winter on the bleak New England shore. It contains also Winslow's account of four expeditions to the Indian tribes about them, and a sermon preached to the Pilgrims by Robert Cushman during his first visit to the colony. For the satisfaction of those Englishmen who had risked their money in the venture, these papers were sent back to England in the second ship that came over. In 1622 they were published anonymously, without the knowledge of the writers, in a small volume called "Mourt's Relation." There was little interest in the subject, and the book soon fell into oblivion, from which it was rescued only during the present century. Thanks to the Massachusetts Historical Society, we have now a second edition, which in type, spelling, and punctuation is an exact reproduction of the first.

"Bradford's Letter Book" contained an invaluable collection of letters to different members of the colony from friends in England and from those left behind in Leyden, together with the replies of the colonists and copies of important documents. The Bradford family allowed it to be placed for safe keeping in the tower of the Old South Church in Boston, where the Rev. Mr. Prince had collected a valuable library on New England history. At the beginning of the Revolution, when the British soldiers took possession of the Old South Church, and turned it into a riding school, many valuable manuscripts were purloined from the library, among them being the Letter Book. Twenty years later Mr. James Clark, of Boston, discovered a remnant of it in a grocer's shop in Nova Scotia. Three hundred and thirty-eight pages had already been used for wrapping-paper. Mr. Clark rescued the remainder, and it was printed in the Collections of the Massachusetts Historical Society.

Bradford's manuscript history was also deposited in the library of the Old South, and disappeared with the letters. It had been cited and quoted by Morton, Prince, Mather, and others; but the work itself had never been printed. From these extracts historians realized the value of what they had lost; but for more than seventy years no trace of it could be found. In 1855 Mr. Barry found in an English book a passage which was ascribed to a manuscript history of Plymouth, in the library of the Bishop of London. He recognized the passage as one of those extracts from Bradford, and began to hope that this manuscript was the long-lost history. Careful examination proved beyond a doubt that the manuscript was Bradford's history, written with his own hand. On one of the blank leaves was this memorandum:—

"This book was rit by goefner William Bradford, and gifen to his son, mager William Bradford, and by him to his son mager John Bradford, rit by me Samuel Bradford, March 20, 1705." Another page contained a note by Rev. Mr. Prince, explaining how the book came into the Old South library.

The Bishop of London allowed a copy to be made for the Massachusetts Historical Society; and this, too, has been printed in their Collections. The original manuscript, however, still remains in the library of the Bishop of London. It is an example of the irony of fate that the palace once occupied by Bancroft, whose cruelty drove the Pilgrims out of England, and later by, Laud, whose tyranny caused the settlement of Massachusetts Bay, should become the repository of the only record of the persecutions, sufferings, and achievements of the exiles. It has been suggested by a prominent Englishman that it would be a graceful act on the part of Great Britain to restore to the United States this precious manuscript, — the very book of Genesis of the nation.

It is easy to see from the dates given above that only the present generation has had the privilege of hearing the story of the Pilgrims from their own lips. Indeed, before the discovery of "Bradford's History," we had not even a complete list of the passengers of the "Mayflower." Prince had copied from Bradford the names of the men who signed the compact, and had indicated by a figure after each name the size of the man's family; but the names of the women and children, whose heroism was equal to if not greater than that of the men, he had not thought it worth while to preserve.

Although the character of Bradford is revealed in every page of his writings, he modestly keeps his personality in the background, speaking of himself only when necessary, and then in an impersonal way. And yet the history of Plymouth contains the entire story of his life. While still a child, he came under the influence of those who were endeavoring to escape from the forms and requirements of the English Church as it was in that day, — the "bare and beggarly ceremonies," as he calls them. His only relatives or guardians were two old uncles, who laughed at his piety and scorned his associates.

The lad's chosen friend and companion was William Brewster, a man thirty years his senior. His influence on Bradford was of the utmost importance, not only on account of his piety, but because of his great stores of wisdom and experience. Brewster was a scholar; but he had seen much of courts and cities, and had studied the world as well as books, before he settled down at Scrooby. In his earlier life he had been for years the trusted secretary and friend of Davison, the Secretary of State to Queen Elizabeth. Davison treated him "rather as a son than a servant." Brewster had been with him at Court and in foreign lands, had been entrusted with important commissions, and had come into very close touch with the mysteries of royalty; for it was Davison, his employer, who signed the death

THE FATHER OF AMERICAN HISTORY. 19

warrant of Mary, Queen of Scots, and lost his office thereby, through Elizabeth's treachery.

Later Brewster received the government post which his father had held, and came to live in the old manor house at Scrooby, under the roof which had sheltered Cardinal Wolsey in his last days. Here he became the "special stay and help" of the little flock of Separatists who were under the ministry of Pastor Clifton and the Rev. John Robinson. When persecution obliged them to give up their place of worship, the congregation assembled regularly at the old manor house, where Brewster, "with great love, entertained them when they came, making provision for them to his great charge." Those who speak of Bradford's lack of early advantages forget that the constant companionship of a man like William Brewster was in itself a liberal education.

The congregation to which Brewster and

Bradford belonged were not long allowed to assemble peaceably in the manor house. Informers were plenty; and they were hunted and persecuted on every side, says Bradford, "so as their former afflictions were but as flea-bitings in comparison of these which now came upon them. For some were taken and clapt up in prison, and others had their houses besett and watcht night and day, and hardly escaped their hands; and ye most were faine to flie and leave their howses and habitations, and the means of their livelehood. Seeing themselves thus molested, and that ther was no hope of their continuance ther, by a joynte consente they resolved to goe into ye Low-Countries, wher they heard was freedome of Religion for all men.

"Being thus constrained to leave their native soyle and countrie, their lands and livings, and all their friends and familiar acquaintance, it was much, and thought marvelous by many. But to go into a countrie they knew not (but by hearsay,) wher they must learn a new language, and get their livings they knew not how, it being a dear place, and subject to ye misseries of warr, it was by many thought an adventure almost desperate, a case intolerable, and a misserie worse then death. Especially seeing they were not acquainted with trads nor traffique, (by which yt countrie doth subsiste) but had only been used to a plaine countrie life, and ye innocente trade of husbandry. But these things did not dismay them (though they did sometimes trouble them) for their desires were sett on ye ways of God, and to injoye his ordinances; but they rested on his providence, and knew whom they had beleeved."

Yet this was not all, continues Bradford; for though they could not stay, yet were they not suffered to go. The ports and havens were closed against them; they were obliged to steal away like criminals, to bribe the mariners, and give "exterordinarie" rates for their passages, and were many times betrayed and surprised and intercepted, and "thereby put to great trouble and charge." At one time, when they had chartered a ship which was to meet them at Boston, forty miles from Scrooby, the master of the ship betrayed them. As soon as the victims were on board, the officers appeared and hurried them ashore. After robbing and maltreating them, they threw them into prison. The majority were released in a few weeks; but Bradford, Brewster, and five others "of ye principall" were kept in prison for some time. Bradford was at this time only eighteen years of age, but was, as we see, one "of ye principall."

The next year another attempt was made. This time they engaged a "Dutchman at Hull" who had a ship of his own. A few of the men were on board his boat, waiting to receive the women and children and their goods from the little bark which had brought them, when a company of officers appeared. The cowardly Dutch captain at once put to sea, without waiting for the rest of his passengers. Those strong men wept. They begged to be put ashore that they might protect their families and their possessions, but in vain. They were carried out to sea; and after a terrible storm, which took them nearly a thousand miles out of their way, they were landed in Holland. Here Bradford was arrested as a fugitive from English justice and put in prison, but was released when it was found he was only a religious exile.

After many other disappointments and mishaps "they all gatt over at length, some at one time and some at another, and some in one place and some in another, and mette togeather againe according to their desires, with no small rejoycing.

"Being now come into ye Low Countries, they saw many goodly and fortified cities, strongly walled and garded with troopes of armed men. Also they heard a strange and uncouth language, and beheld ye differente maners and custumes of ye people, with their strange fashions and attires; all so farre differing from yt of their plaine countrie villages (wherin they were bred, and had so longe lived) as it seemed they were come into a new world. But these were not ye things they much looked on, or long tooke up their thoughts; for they had other work in hand, and another kind of warr to wage and maintaine. For though they saw faire and bewtifull cities, flowing with abundance of all sorts of welth and riches, yet it was not longe before they saw the grime and grisly face of povertie coming upon them like an armed man, with whom they must bukle and incounter, and from whom they could not flye; but they were armed with faith and patience against him and all his encounters; and though they were sometimes foyled, yet by God's assistance they prevailed and got ye victorie."

Those among them who had been men of property had expended their wealth for the common good. The great expense of bringing over the whole number, together with the losses and misfortunes which had attended their efforts, had swallowed up their fortunes, so that all were now upon the same footing, — obliged to earn their living in whatever way they could. Bradford apprenticed himself to a weaver; others became hatters, wool-combers, spinners, carpenters, brewers, bakers, tailors, and masons.

They remained, however, but a few months in Amsterdam, fearing to become involved in the fierce controversy which was raging between the two English churches already there. Hence they resolved to remove to Leyden, although the opportunities for earning a livelihood were less favorable. They valued "peace and their spirituall comforte above any other riches whatsoever. And at length they came to raise a competente and comforteable living, but with hard and continuall labor."

The Rev. John Robinson, their pastor, was a "common father to them all," in temporal as well as spiritual affairs. He was a man rarely gifted for the place he was called to fill. His learning and talents finally brought him into such notice that the freedom of the university was extended to him. Among the privileges and perquisites belonging to this honor were "exemption from municipal control, half a tun of beer every month, and ten gallons of wine every three months." William Brewster was chosen as assistant pastor and elder.

Brewster, however, suffered especial hardships. He had spent all of his fortune for the common good, and being, by his age and former manner of life, unfitted for the trades and callings which the Pilgrims were forced to take up, he had great difficulty to support his large family. But his cheerfulness and dignity never failed him. At length he obtained employment in teaching English to some German and Danish students at the university, using Latin as a means of communication. He invented a text-book on the plan of the Latin grammar, and attained some celebrity as a teacher. Afterward he set up a printing-press, bringing out a number of theological books which could not safely be published in England. The English government demanded his arrest, but he escaped by flight.

In the course of years many new members were added to the little congregation, from different parts of England, and Bradford says they were sometimes not fewer than three hundred communicants. They lived in Leyden eleven or twelve years, in such peace and harmony that the Dutch magistrates held them up as an example to the French Walloons, who also had a church there but who were of a less peaceable disposition.

At length, however, the wiser members of the flock began to talk of removal to some other place. "Not out of any newfangledness, or other such like giddie humor, by which men are oftentimes transported to their great hurt and danger, but for sundrie weightie and solid reasons."

First, the difficulty of obtaining a living; for many that would come to them were unable to endure the labor and hard fare, "yea, some even preferred and chose ye prisons in England rather than this libertie in Holland with these afflictions."

Secondly, though the people generally bore these difficulties very cheerfully, yet old age began to steal on many of them, and they saw that they must soon scatter, or sink under their burdens.

Thirdly, "as necessitie was a task-master over them they were forced to be such to their children," and many of them were overtaxed physically and growing old before their time.

"But that which was more lamentable, and of all sorrowes most heavie to be borne, was that many of their children, by these occasions, and ye great licentiousness of youth in yt countrie, and ye manifold temptations of the place, were drawne away by evill examples into extravagante and dangerous courses, getting ye raines off their neks, and departing from their parents. Some became souldiers, others tooke upon them farr viages by sea, and other some worse courses, tending to dissolutenes and the danger of their souls, to ye great greefe of their parents and dishonour of God. So that they saw their posteritie would be in danger to degenerate and be corrupted."

Lastly, the hope of laying some foundation for propagating the gospel in heathen lands. For these reasons and others they resolved to leave Leyden and to form a colony in some place where they could remain Englishmen and train up their children in their own church. Their thoughts turned to America as the only land offering room for their plans. Some, won by the glowing accounts of Sir Walter Raleigh, were for settling in Guiana; but the unsuitable climate, and the fact that Spain laid claim to the region, were sufficient objections. Others moved to join the English colony already established in Virginia. But it was feared that the church could not enjoy in Virginia the independence it desired. Those who had given most thought to the subject preferred a location farther north, yet still under the jurisdiction of the Virginia Company, as it was called.

Several unsuccessful attempts had been made to plant a colony in this northern latitude, but in each case the colonists had given up, and had returned to England with the most disheartening reports of the country. Those who now objected to the scheme did not allow the promoters of it to forget or ignore the dangers and difficulties to be faced. They not only urged the perils of the sea, the length and discomfort of the voyage, the change of climate, the liability to famine and sickness, but added, that "those which should escape or overcome these difficulties, should yett be in continuall danger of ye salvage people, who are cruell, barbarous and most trecherous, being most furious in their rage, and merciles wher they overcome; not being contente only to kill, and take away life, but delight to tormente men in ye most bloodie manner that may be; fleaing some alive with ye shells of fishes, cutting of ye members and joynts of others by peesmeale, and broiling on ye coles, eate ye collops of their flesh in their sight whilst they live; with other cruelties horrible to be related. And surely it could not be thought but ye very hearing of these things could not but move ye very bowels of men to grate within them, and make ye weake to quake and tremble." In spite of all this they did not abandon the design.

For nearly two years three of their principal men were busy in England making arrangements for the emigration. There were two joint stock companies whose business was the colonization of America, and from one of these they obtained a grant of land, the place to be chosen by themselves somewhere near the mouth of the Delaware. They endeavored also to obtain a charter from King James with the privilege of religious liberty. But the most the king could be brought to promise was that he would connive at their going, and would not molest them so long as they conducted themselves peaceably. Many were frightened at this, and afraid to venture without a charter; but Bradford wisely saw that if the king's word was not good neither would his seal be, for if he desired to wrong them he could do it "though they had a seal as broad as ye house flore."

Arrangements were finally made with seventy "merchant adventurers" in London, who were to furnish the capital for the enterprise, while the settlers were to mortgage their labor for seven years, during which time all profits and benefits "gott by trade, traffick, trucking, working, fishing, or any other means of any person or persons," were to be turned into the common fund. At the end of seven years the capital and profits, the houses, lands, goods, and chattels, were to be divided equally between the adventurers and planters. The colonists found some of the conditions very hard. They had hoped to reserve two days in the week for themselves, "for their own private imployment." They also felt that the homes which they should build in a new country ought to belong to them at the end of the seven years instead of being divided with the adventurers. But both of these clauses were stricken out of the agreement, greatly to their disappointment.

When these things had been settled, they appointed a solemn public fast to ask further guidance of the Lord as to who should go. There was not money enough to transport the whole company, nor could all have been ready to go at once. It was therefore resolved that the younger and stronger members should go first, but only such as should freely offer themselves; those who remained promising to join them as soon as possible, if the Lord gave them life, means, and opportunity. Pastor Robinson was to remain with the congregation at Leyden, and Elder Brewster to accompany the Pilgrims to the New World.

In the number who were to go were some who were but recent additions to the flock; among others, Edward Winslow, a talented and educated young Englishman, who, passing through Holland three years before, had been so charmed with the little community that he joined himself to it. He was now ready to accompany them in this perilous undertaking; and he it was who became their tongue, their ever ready ambassador, whether to savage tribes or to English courts. Another recent accession was the doughty little captain, Miles Standish, who was not a member of their church, and was even strongly suspected by some of secret leanings toward Roman Catholicism. Whatever his religion, he cast in his lot with the Pilgrims, and proved himself their brave defender in many an hour of terror.

At length all things were in readiness for the departure. A small ship — the "Speedwell" — was brought, which was to carry them to Southampton, where they were to meet the larger vessel which had been procured for them, — the "Mayflower." The smaller ship was to carry a part of them across the Atlantic, and remain with them for a year. Another solemn fast was kept, the pastor taking for his text Ezra viii. 21 :

"And ther at ye river by Ahava, I proclaimed a fast, that we might humble ourselves before our God, and seeke of him a right way for us, and for our children and for all our substance."

"Upon which," says Bradford, "he spente a good part of ye day very profitably. The rest of the time was spente in pouring out prairs to ye Lord with great fervencie, mixed with abundance of tears. And ye time being come that they must departe, they were accompanied with most of their brethren out of the citie, unto a town sundrie miles off called Delfes-Haven, wher the ship lay ready to receive them. *So they lefte yt goodly and pleasant citie, which had been ther resting place near twelve years, but they knew they were pilgrimes, and looked not much on those things, but lift up their eyes to ye heaveus, their dearest countrie, and quieted their spirits.*" Bradford, who writes these words, was leaving behind him his only child, a boy not more than six years old.

"When they came to ye place they found ye ship and all things ready; and such of their freinds as could not come with them followed after them and sundrie also came from Amsterdame to see them shipte and to take their leave of them. That night was spent with litle sleepe by ye most, but with freindly entertainmente and christian discourse and other real expressions of true christian love. The next day, the wind being, faire, they wente aborde and their freinds with them, where truly dolful was ye sight of that sad and mournfull parting; to see what sighs and sobbs and praires did sound amongst them, what tears did gush from every eye, and pithy speeches peirst each harte; that sundry of ye Dutch strangers yt stood on ye key as spectators, could not refraine from tears. Yet comfortable and sweete it was to see shuch lively and true expressions of dear and unfained love. But ye tide (which stays for no man) caling them away yt were thus loath to departe, their Reverend pastor falling downe on his knees (and they all with him) with watrie cheeks comended them with most fervente praiers to the Lord and his blessing. And then with mutuall imbrases and many tears, they tooke their leaves one of another; — which proved to be ye last leave to many of them." This was the embarkation of the Pilgrims.

At Southampton they found the "Mayflower," with those who were to join them there. But they met with serious delays and provocations in their final arrangements with the adventurers. At length, on the fifteenth of August, they "sett sayle." The passengers were divided, ninety being assigned to the "Mayflower" and thirty to the "Speedwell." They had not gone far when the master of the smaller ship complained that his ship was leaking, and that he dared not go farther. Both vessels resolved to put into Dartmouth to have the "Speedwell" searched and mended, which was done, "to their great charg and losse of time and a faire winde." They again put to sea, but had gone only three hundred miles from Land's End when the master of the small ship again complained of his leaky vessel, declaring he could hardly keep her free by constant pumping. After consultation both ships put back to Plymouth.

No leak could be discovered in the "Speedwell;" but concluding that she was unseaworthy from general weakness, they decided to send her back to London, and continue the voyage with only one vessel. This necessitated leaving a part of the passengers; for they could not all be crowded into the "Mayflower."

"The which (though it was greevous and caused great discouragmente) was put into execution. So after they had tooke out such provission as ye other ship could well stow, and concluded both what number and what persons to send bak, they made another sad parting, ye one ship going backe for London, and ye other was to proceede on her viage. Those that went bak were for the most parte such as were willing so to doe, either out of some discontente, or feare they conceived of ye ill success of ye vioage, seeing so many croses befall, and the year time so farr spente; but others, in regarde of their own weaknes, and charge of many yonge children, were thought least usefull, and most unfite to bear ye brunte of this hard adventure; unto which worke of God, and judgemente of their brethren, they were contented to submite. And thus, like Gedeon's armie, this small number was devided, as if ye Lord by this worke of his providence thought these few too many for ye great worke he had to do." Afterward it was learned that the master of the "Speedwell" had repented of his agreement to remain a year with the colonists, and had deceived them.

Eighteen of the company were sent back to London in the "Speedwell." The remaining one hundred and two were crowded into the " Mayflower; " and they put to sea for the third time on the sixteenth of September. By the treachery and mismanagement of others they had been robbed of six weeks of fair weather, and the journey had been pushed into the most unfavorable season of the year. In mid-ocean they encountered terrible storms, by which the ship was "shrewdly shaken," and the main beam amidships "bowed and cracked." The frightened sailors began to talk of returning, and would probably have done so had not Europe been as far away as America. Fortunately one of the passengers had brought from Holland a great iron jack-screw; and with this the beam was crowded home. One of the passengers died at sea; but their number remained the same, for Mistress Hopkins gave birth to a boy, who received the appropriate name of Oceanus.

On the twentieth of November, at break of day, they espied land, and the appearance of it much comforted them. It proved to be Cape Cod; and as their patent gave them no authority to settle there, they turned the ship southward, toward the mouth of the Hudson. But the difficulties and dangers of the passage, and the fierce opposition of the captain, forced them to return to Cape Cod harbor, and to think of a settlement there. "Being thus arrived in a good harbor and brought safe to land, they fell upon their knees and blessed ye God of heaven, who had brought them over ye vast and furious ocean, and delivered them from all ye perils and miseries therof, againe to set their feete on the firme and stable earth, their proper element.

"But hear," says Bradford, "I cannot but stay and make a pause, and stand half amased at this poore peoples presente condition; and so I thinke will the reader too, when he well considers the same. Being thus passed ye vast ocean, and a sea of troubles before in their preparation (as may be remembered by yt which wente before) they had now no freinds to wellcome them, nor inns to entertaine or refresh their weather-beaten bodys, no houses or much less townes to repair too, to seeke for succoure. It is recorded in scripture as a mercie to ye apostle and his ship wraked company, yt the barbarians showed them no small kindness in refreshing them, but these savage barbarians, when they mette with them (as after will appeare) were readier to fill their sids full of arrows then otherwise. And for ye season it was winter, and they that know ye winters of yt countrie know them to be sharp and violent, and subject to cruell and feirce storms, deangerous to travill to known places, much more to serch an unknown coast. Besides, what could they see but a hidious and desolate wildernes, full of wild beasts and wild men? and what multitudes ther might be of them they knew not. Nether could they, as it were, goe up to the top of Pisgah, to vew from this willdernes a more goodly countrie to feed their hops; for which way soever they turned their eyes (save upward to ye heavens) they could have little solace or content in respecte of any outward objects. For summer being done, all things stand upon them with a wetherbeaten face; and ye whole countrie, full of woods and thickets, represented a wild and savage heiw. If they looked behind them, there was ye mighty ocean which they had passed, and was now as a main barr and goulfe to separate them from all the civill parts of ye world. If it be said they had a ship to succoure them, it is trew; but what heard they daly from the master and company? but that with speed they should look out a place with their shallop. Yea, it was muttered by some, that if they gott not a place in time, they would turn them and their goods ashore and leave them. What could now sustain them but ye spirite of God and his grace? May not and ought not the children of these fathers rightly to say: *Our faithers were Englishmen which came over this great ocean, and were ready to perish in this wilderness; but they cried unto ye Lord and he heard their voyce and looked on their adversitie. Let them therfore praise ye Lord, because he is good and his mercies endure for ever.*"

The passage from Plymouth to Cape Cod had lasted sixty-seven days, but from Southampton it had been ninety-nine days, while those who started from Delft haven had been more than four months on shipboard. They must still be content in midwinter with those narrow, uncomfortable quarters, and for the women and children there were many weeks of waiting before all could be provided for on shore.

The place where they now were was wholly outside the jurisdiction of the Virginia Company. Therefore the patent which it had cost them so much trouble to procure was useless. They had no doubt of being able to obtain a patent from the other company; but in the mean time another trouble arose. Not all the passengers of the "Mayflower" were saints by any means. Not all of them were even desirable citizens, as later events proved. Their relations to the adventurers had obliged the Pilgrims to allow certain persons, of whom they knew nothing, to join them in England. From some of these strangers troublesome and mutinous mutterings were now heard, to the effect that when they came ashore they would have their own liberty; since the patent was null, and they had no charter, there was no authority to which they need be subject; as soon as they landed every man would be his own master. For this reason, and in accordance with

Robinson's advice that they should at once frame a form of civil polity, forty-one men met in the little cabin of the "Mayflower" and signed the famous compact: "In the name of God, amen. We, whose names are underwritten, the loyal subjects of our dread sovereign lord King James, by the grace of God of Great Britain, France and Ireland, King, Defender of the Faith, etc., having undertaken for the glory of God and the advancement of the Christian faith, and honor of our King and country, a voyage to plant the first colony in the northern parts of Virginia, do, by these presents solemnly and mutually, in the presence of God, and one of another, covenant and combine ourselves together into a civil body politic, for our better ordering and preservation and furtherance of the ends aforesaid; and by virtue hereof to enact, constitute, and frame such just and equal laws, ordinances, acts, constitutions, and offices, from time to time, as shall be thought most meet and convenient for the general good of the colony, unto which we promise all due submission and obedience. In witness whereof we have hereunder subscribed our names at Cape Cod, the Eleventh of November, (Old Style) in the year of the reign of our sovereign lord King James, of England, France and Ireland, the eighteenth, and of Scotland the fifty-fourth-Anno Dom., 1620."

"This," said John Quincy Adams, "is perhaps the only instance in human history of that positive, original social compact which speculative philosophers have imagined as the only legitimate source of government. Here was a unanimous and personal assent by all the individuals of the community to the association, by which they became a nation." The malcontents, whoever they were, signed the compact with the rest; so that all had pledged themselves to be bound by such laws as the majority should adopt.

After this they elected Mr. John Carver governor for that year.

Two days later the women of the "Mayflower" took decisive action. They insisted upon being carried ashore to do a "much needed washing." Monday, the twenty-third of November, deserves to be remembered in the annals of history as the first "wash day" in New England.

The ship was now anchored about a mile from the site of Provincetown. The men got out the shallop which they had brought from England, "stowed away in the ship's quarters," and set the carpenters to repairing it, in order that they might explore the coast to find a suitable site for a town. Too impatient to wait for the shallop, sixteen men, under command of Capt. Miles Standish, made an expedition on foot. They were gone three days, and brought back some Indian corn, "which seemed to them a very goodly sight, they never having seen such before." This corn was used for seed-corn, and proved the salvation of the colony. While they were absent, an addition had been made to the colony by the birth of Peregrine White, the first English child born on the coast of New England.

The second expedition was made with the shallop, but they returned discouraged, having found no suitable spot. While they lay at anchor in Cape Cod harbor, the whole company came near being blown into eternity by the ubiquitous small boy, from whom not even the "Mayflower" was exempt. John Billington, having found a loaded gun, shot it off in the cabin, where there was a keg of loose powder not four feet from the fire. "And yet, by God's mercy, no harm done," says Bradford, mildly.

On the sixteenth of December, ten of the men, with eight seamen, again started out in the shallop to find a larger harbor, although it was so cold that the sea spray froze on their clothes, making them like coats of iron. The second night some of the party built a barricade, and slept on shore. In the morning they had their first unpleasant encounter with the Indians, who showered arrows upon them from behind the trees. Fortunately no one was hurt, though some coats hanging on the barricade were shot through and through. Having frightened the Indians away with their firearms, and gathered up eighteen arrows to send back to England, they returned to their boat.

In the afternoon a storm came on them, with sleet and snow; the sea grew rough, the rudder broke, their mast split in three pieces, the sail fell overboard, the pilot lost his head entirely, and they would all have been cast away but for the presence of mind of one of the sailors. "Though it was very dark and rained sore, yet in ye end they gott under the lee of a small iland, and remained there all yt night in saftie. But they did not know it to be an island, and some were afraid to go ashore for fear of the Indians." Others were so weak and cold and wet that they could not endure it, but got ashore and built a fire. After midnight the wind changed to the northwest, it froze hard, and all were glad to come ashore. "Ye next day was a faire, sunshinig day, and they found them sellvs to be on an iland, secure from ye Indeans, wher they might drie their stufe, fixe their peeces, rest themselves, and gave God thanks for his mercies in their manifould deliverances. And this being the last day of ye weeke, they prepared ther to keepe ye Sabath." *On the Sabbath Day they rested.* When we remember their situation, — the cold winter day, so far from the ship, on an unknown island, with no shelter over their heads, their families anxiously awaiting their return, — when we consider all this, and see these men quietly keeping the Sabbath on Clark's Island, we can form some estimate of their respect for the day. That there could be any combination of circumstances which would justify "breaking the Sabbath" seems never to have entered their minds. In this connection it is of interest to note their record of Christmas a few days later: "We went on shore, some to fell timber, some to saw, some to rive, and some to carry; so no man rested all that day." Christmas was to them a relic of popery; but the Sabbath day was sacred.

On Monday they sounded the harbor, and found it fit for shipping; they marched into the land, and found diverse cornfields and little running brooks, — a place very good for situation. This, then, was the landing of the Pilgrims, "the birthday of New England." The spot which they had chosen had the four advantages of which they had been in search, — a harbor for ships, cleared land, good water, and natural defences. Long before, by a singular coincidence, the place had received from Capt. John Smith the name of Plymouth, — the name of the last port in England from which they had sailed. The exploring party had been absent about a week, and their families in the "Mayflower" were eagerly awaiting their return. "So they returned to their shipe againe with this news to ye rest of their people, which did much comforte their harts."

William Bradford was one of the exploring party. On his return to the ship, weary and worn from exposure, but glad to be the bearer of good news, he was met by the terrible tidings that the young wife who had accompanied him across the ocean had fallen overboard and drowned during his absence. The home of which he was dreaming in the lovely spot which they had chosen would be a lonely one for him.

By the end of the week the "Mayflower" was safely anchored in Plymouth harbor, her journey done, her name made immortal.

Another Sabbath Day the Pilgrims rested in sight of the "promised land." Then, the majority having confirmed the choice of the ten explorers, they set to work to build a town out of the raw material. They had to hew the logs, carry stone, make mortar, and cut thatch. On the hill above they planned to build a platform for their cannon, to protect them from the Indians, whose dusky forms they could see now and then sulking about among the trees.

Another hill was chosen for a burying-ground; for so many were the dead and dying that this was one of their first needs. A common house was built, twenty feet square, to receive their provisions, and to shelter those who had begun to sleep on the shore. In order to do away with the necessity of building many houses, the company was divided into nineteen families; and each single man was assigned to some family.

A street was laid out, running from the

harbor to the hill, parallel with the little stream which they called Town Brook. The choice of location was determined by lot, and homesteads were staked out on each side of the way. The street was at first called simply "The Street;" afterward, when there were others, it was called First Street. Two hundred years later it received its present name of Leyden Street. It is still there; and as we pass between the two rows of houses, along the path so often trodden by the Pilgrims, "from the seaside to the hill, . . . he is cold indeed who does not feel the thrill that comes from treading on hallowed ground."

The building went but slowly. "Frost and foul weather hindered them much." Seldom could they work more than half the week. Much time was lost in going to and from the ship; for only a few of them could sleep in the "common house." The ship lay a mile and a half from the shore; and they often had to wait for the tide. Could we linger over every step of the building of the town, could we follow day by day Bradford's photographic record of the doings of the Pilgrims during these first weeks, we should find every page full of interest, full of quaint and pathetic incidents. There was that terribly anxious night when two of their number, who had gone to cut thatch, were lost in the woods, and stood all night listening to the howling of the wolves, trying to keep their two dogs from answering the howls, and ready to climb the trees at a moment's warning if the wolves should approach near. Thus they waited for daylight with the very blood freezing in their veins. Then who can forget that afternoon walk of John Goodman and his little spaniel? The dog, chased by the wolves, crouched for protection between his master's frozen feet. Goodman, with no weapon but a stick, tried to frighten away the wolves, " which sat on their tails grinning at him."

After three weeks' labor, their common house being finished and covered with a roof of thatch, they prepared to observe the Sabbath there. All who were able to leave the ship were to attend the services. But on Sunday morning, when those on shipboard turned their eyes as usual toward their future home, they saw the common house in flames. They supposed the fire to be the work of savages; and they waited in trembling uncertainty until the tide would permit them to go ashore and learn the fate of their brethren. They found that the fire had caught from a spark, that only the roof had burned, and that no one was injured, although Governor Carver and William Bradford had lain sick in the house with their loaded muskets by their sides.

"In these hard and difficulte beginings they found some discontents and murmurings arise amongst some, and mutinous speeches and carriags in other; but they were soone quelled and overcome by ye wisdome, patience, and just and equall carrage of things by ye Governor and better part, which clave faithfully together in ye maine. But that which was most sadd and lamentable was, that in two or three months time halfe of their company dyed, espetially in January and February, being ye depth of winter, and wanting houses and other comforts; being infected with ye scurvie and other diseases, which this long vioyage and their inaccommodate condition had brought upon them; so as ther dyed sometimes two or three of a day, in ye aforesaid time; that of one hundred and odd persons, scarce fifty remained. And of these in ye time of most distress, there was but six or seven sound persons, who, to their great comendations be it spoken, spared no pains, night nor day, but with abundance of toyle and hazard of their owne health, fetched them woode, made them fires, drest them meat, made their beads, washed their lothsome cloaths, cloathed and uncloathed them; in a word, did all ye homly and necessarie offices for them which dainty and quesie stomacks cannot endure to hear named; and all this willingly and cherfully, without any grudging in ye least, shewing herein their true love unto their freinds and bretheren. A rare example and worthy to be remembered. Tow of these seven were Mr. William Brewster, ther Reverend Elder, and Miles Standish, ther Captein and military commander, unto whom myselfe, and many others were much beholden in our low and sicke condition. And yet the Lord so upheld these persons, as in this generall calamity, they were not at all infected."

We have many instances of Elder Brewster's greatness of heart; but we are glad to have this picture of Miles Standish nursing the sick, — glad to know that underneath that fiery temper and warlike spirit was a nature as tender and gentle as a woman's. Rose Standish, his delicate wife, was one of the first to droop and die in the unkind air of New England. The graves upon the hillside had grown so numerous that they were obliged to smooth away all traces of them and sow the place with grain, through fear lest the Indians should see how their numbers had been reduced and take advantage of their weakness.

One of the first steps which the Pilgrims took was to hold a town meeting, and form a military organization, electing Miles Standish as their commander. In the beginning the number of men had been but forty-one, of whom a large proportion had already sickened and died, so that their standing army was a small one. Captain Standish could boast, as did Cæsar, that he knew the name of every man in his army. Yet he yielded not an inch of his authority, but insisted upon strict military discipline and obedience.

"John Billington, for his contempt of the Captain's lawful command with opprobrious speeches, was convented before the whole company and adjudged to have his neck and heels tied together, but upon his humbling himself and craving pardon he was released."

During all this time they had had no communication with the natives, although they could see one now and then skulking behind a tree. One day in March, a dusky savage, naked save for a leather girdle about his waist, passed up the street to the common house, where the men were holding a town meeting, and greeted them with the word "Welcome." His name was Samoset; and he had learned some English words from the men who came to fish on the coast of Maine. From him they learned that the place where they were was called by the Indians Pawtucket, and that four years before a terrible plague had exterminated the tribe which dwelt there. Samoset was well received, and came again and again, the third time bringing word that Massasoit, the grand sachem of the tribes of Pokanoket, wanted to visit them. When the chief appeared with twenty warriors, they received him with as much pomp and state as they could summon. Captain Standish with six musketeers met him at Town Brook, and conducted him to a house where a green rug and cushion had been placed for him. Then Governor Carver appeared with a small body-guard of musketeers, attended by drum and trumpet. This visit was of the gravest importance. A treaty was concluded with Massasoit which was not broken for more than forty years. He also undertook to convey to the other tribes the peaceable intentions of the white men.

Samoset had brought with him Squanto, or Tisquantum, the sole surviving Indian of the tribe which had been exterminated. Squanto's life had been saved in a curious manner. Some seven years previously Captain Hunt, one of John Smith's men, having beguiled a score of Indians into his ship under pretence of trading, carried them off to Spain, and sold them as slaves. Squanto was one of the number. He was taken to England, where he learned the language and something of English habits. After three or four years he was carried back to America by Captain Dermer, to find himself the sole survivor of his tribe. Squanto became, as it were, the guest of the colony, remaining with them as long as he lived, and proving of great service as an interpreter. He also taught them how to sow and tend their corn, and where to hunt and fish. Captain Hunt's treachery had aroused in the Indians a feeling of hatred toward all white men; and when they saw the colonists coming, they looked upon them as enemies. They held an assembly in a " dark and dismal swampe, . . . where they got all the *Powachs* of ye country," says Bradford, "for three days togeather, in a horid and divellish maner to curse and execrate them with their conjurations." The treaty with Massasoit was therefore a gain of no small importance.

At length the weary winter wore away. "Warm and fair weather appeared and the birds sang in the trees most pleasantly. . . . It pleased God the mortalitie begane to cease amongst them, and ye sick and lame recovered apace, which put as it were new life into them; though they had borne their sadd affliction with much patience and contentednes, as I thinke any people could doe."

There was no necessity now for the nineteen houses they had planned to build. A much smaller number would suffice. Half the company had found a home in the "house not made with hands." Many, many times had the sad pilgrimage been made to the hill which they had chosen for a burial-ground. And now, with the approach of spring, another trial was before them. The "Mayflower," which had remained in the harbor through the winter, was to return to England. The crew, as we know, were coarse, inhuman men. The captain had shown the Pilgrims scant courtesy. The occasions when they were "kindly and friendly together" had been rare enough to be worthy of special mention. Yet, with all that, it was a sad day when the old ship sailed away. She was the only connecting link between the Pilgrims and the civilized world. With her departure all possibility of return, all means of communication were cut off. They might be destroyed by the Indians or swept away by disease, and none would know their fate. Five hundred miles to the north of them were a few Frenchmen. Five hundred miles to the south was the little colony of Jamestown. But practically all the white people on the continent were as far removed from them as if they had been in Europe. The Pilgrims were surrounded by savage tribes, of which only one had signified peaceable intentions. Yet, in the face of all these discouragements, when the "Mayflower" sailed away not one of the Pilgrims was on board. Surely the words which Brewster had written were true: "It is not with us as with other men, whom small things can discourage, or small discontentments cause to wish themselves at home again."

Soon after the departure of the "Mayflower" the colony suffered a great loss in the death of Governor Carver. He returned from the field, where he had gone to labor with the others, prostrated with the heat, and died a few days later. They buried him in "great lamentation and heaviness, with as much solemnity as they were in capacity to perform, with a discharge of some volleys of shot of all that bare arms." His wife, overcome with grief, followed him in a few weeks. The first governor of Plymouth left no descendants.

William Bradford was chosen as Carver's successor; and from that time until his death, thirty-six years later, the colony looked upon him as its head. "Five times he by importunity gat off, insisting that if the office of governor were an honor others ought to share it, and if it were a burden all ought to help to bear it." He succeeded in having Winslow serve three years, and Prince two. For thirty-one years Bradford served them faithfully as governor; and though the colony was small, the duties of the office were not light. He was required to be chief justice, minister of foreign affairs, and auditor of the treasury. There were also many lesser matters to which he was obliged to give his attention. For instance, when famine threatened, and the stock of grain was so reduced that they restricted themselves to a quarter of a pound of bread a day for each person, the governor caused it to be given out daily, "otherwise, had it been in their own custodie, they would have eate it up and then starved." The governor also worked with them in the fields, and led out the men to their work every morning.

At the town meetings, not only had military order been adopted, but also such civil laws and ordinances as were thought "behooveful for their present estate and condition." Soon after Bradford's election occurred the second offence requiring punishment. Two young men became engaged in a quarrel, and having brought over some Old World ideas, decided to settle it by a duel. With a sword in the right hand and a dagger in the left they fought until each had received a slight wound, and their honor was satisfied. But not so the honor of the colony. The Pilgrims considered it a disgrace; and the duellists were sentenced to lie in a public place, neck and heels tied together, for twenty-four hours. The punishment was begun; but after an hour or two of suffering the culprits pleaded so earnestly that they were released. The treatment proved effectual; for this was the first and last duel fought in the "old colony."

The first summer of Bradford's administration proved a busy one. Twenty-six acres were planted and tilled, — six in barley, wheat, and peas, and twenty or more in corn. By the advice of Squanto two or three herrings were placed in each hill of corn as a fertilizer. When we remember that they had neither horses nor cattle, that all the ground had to be broken up by hand, the many tons of herrings to be transported from Town Brook to the fields, and that their entire force consisted of twenty-one men and six boys, we may form some idea of their labors. At the end of the summer "The Street" contained seven dwelling-houses and four public buildings, — one used for worship and for town meetings, the others as depots for their crops, their provisions, and their trading stock. A fair harvest had been gathered, which with fish, game, and fruit furnished a variety of food. Besides all this, four expeditions had been made to establish peaceable relations with the different tribes of Indians. In view of this general prosperity Governor Bradford appointed a day of Thanksgiving, "that they might after a special manner rejoice together after they had gathered the fruits of their labors." To be neighborly they invited Massasoit, who came, bringing ninety warriors with him. For three days they feasted and entertained this company, rehearsing for their benefit their military tactics and evolutions. Thus the great festival of Thanksgiving was inaugurated in New England, and we are glad to know that wild turkeys were a feature of the feast.

In November, just a year from the time

the Pilgrims first sighted land, another ship arrived, the "Fortune," bringing to the colony an addition of thirty-five members. They were received with open arms, though as they had brought no provisions their arrival was somewhat inopportune. The colonists had prepared for winter; but when they saw the number of mouths almost doubled, they were obliged to put every one upon half rations until spring. The second year famine again "pinched them sore," while the third spring, by the time their corn was planted, " all their victuals were spent, and they were only to rest on God's providence; at night not many times knowing where to have a bite of anything the next day. And so, as one well observed, had need to pray that God would give them their daily bread, above all people in the world." Men were seen at noon-day, staggering for want of food. Elder Brewster, who had dined in palaces, and had often feasted the whole Scrooby congregation in his own house, sat down to his daily dinner of boiled clams and spring water, and thanked God that he and his were still allowed to "suck of the abundance of the seas and of the treasures hid in the sand."

They now began to ask what they should do to raise greater crops of corn wherewith to prevent such misery. After long debate, the governor, with the advice of the chiefest among them, decided to let every man plant his own corn. This year, therefore, they assigned a "parcel of land" to each family for its own use. "This had very good success; for it made all hands very industrious, so as much more corne was planted than otherwaise would have bene, by any means ye governor or any other could use, and saved him a great deall of trouble and gave farr better contente. The women now wente willingly into ye feild and tooke their litle ons with them to set corne which before would aledg weaknes, and inabilitie; whom to have compelled would have bene thought great tiranie and oppression."

Governor Bradford moralizes on this result to the effect that communism is not a success. "The experience that was had in this comone course and condition, tried sundrie years, and that amongst godly and sober men, may well evince the vanitie of that conceite of Platos and other ancients, applauded by some of later times; — that ye taking away of propertie, and bringing in comunitie into a comonewealth, would make them happy and florishing; as if they were wiser then God. For this comunitie, (so farr as it was) was found to breed much confusion and discontent, and retard much imploymet that would have been to their benefite and comforte. For ye yong-men that were most able and fitte for labour and service did repine that they should spend their time and streingth to worke for other men's

wives and children, with out any recompence.
The strong, or man of parts, had no more
in devission of victails and cloaths, then he
that was weake and not able to doe a quarter
ye other could; this was thought injuestice.
The aged and graver men to be ranked and
equalised in labours, and victails, cloaths, etc.,
with ye meaner and yonger sorte, thought it
some indiginitie and disrespect unto them.
And for men's wives to be commanded to doe
service for other men, as dresing their meate,
washing their cloaths, etc., they deemd it a
kind of slaverie, neither could many husbands
well brooke it. . . . And would have bene
worse if they had been men of another condition. Let none objecte this is men's corruption, and nothing to ye course it selfe.
I answer, seeing all men have this corruption
in them, God in his wisdome saw another
course fiter for them."

By the new method a much larger crop
was sown; but for a time their greater in-

dustry and pains seemed in vain. From May to July there was a heavy drought, with such great heat that the corn began to wither away. A day of fasting was appointed, — a day of solemn humiliation and prayer. They assembled in the fortified house on the hill-top, and the services continued some eight or nine hours. When they began the heavens were as clear as ever; but as hour after hour passed by in prayer, the sky began to overcast, and at length came rain "with shuch sweete and gentle showers, as gave them cause of rejoyceing and blessing God. It came, without either wind, or thunder, or any violence, and by degreese in that abundance, as that ye earth was thorowly wete and soked therwith." Winslow says, "It was hard to say whether their withered corn or drooping affections were most quickened or revived." The Indians were greatly impressed by this answer to prayer, particularly by the manner of it; for when their conjurers brought rain, they said, it came in such torrents as to do more harm than good by beating down the crops.

In this year the colony narrowly escaped complete destruction by the Indians. Massasoit, whose life had been saved by Winslow, in his gratitude revealed a plot of the Neponsets to kill every white man on the coast. Standish, by prompt and heroic measures, put an end to the conspiracy, and to all further hostility from the savages for many years.

This same eventful summer arrived two vessels,—the "Anne" and the "Little James,"—bringing a reinforcement to the colony of sixty new members. "Some of them being very usefull persons, and became good members to ye body, and some were ye wives and children of shuch as were hear allready. And some were so bad, as they were faine to be at charge to send them home again ye next year." Besides, there came some that did not belong to the general body, but were "on their particular," as they called it; that is, they were subject to the general government, but were not under contract to the adventurers. These afterward caused trouble and disturbance. The new arrivals had come with high hopes, and great was their disappointment at what they found. "When they saw their low and poore condition a shore, they were much danted and dismayed, and according to their diverse humores were diversly affected; some wished them selves in England againe; others fell a weeping, fancying their own miserie in what they saw now in others; other some pitying the distress they saw their friends had been long in, and still were under; in a word, all were full of sadnes. . . . And truly it was no marvell they should be thus affected, for they were in a very low condition, many were ragged in aparell, and some litle beter than halfe naked. For food, they were all alike. The best dish they could presente their friends with was a lobster, or a peece of fish, without bread or anything els but a cupp of fair spring water. And ye long continuance of this diate and their labours abroad, had something abated ye freshnes of their former complexion."

Among those who came in the "Anne" was Mistress Alice Southworth, who in less than a fortnight became the wife of Governor Bradford, — rather a short courtship, unless we may believe the old tradition that the two had been lovers in England many years before. Miles Standish also found a wife in the "Anne;" and Barbara soon consoled him for the slight put upon him by Priscilla. When the harvest came, the famine was over. "The face of things was changed to the rejoicing of the hearts of many." The result of the individual labor was apparent; for every one had enough for the year, and some of the abler and more industrious had grain to sell. Edward Winslow had returned to England in the "Anne," and the next year he brought back four head of cattle, — "the first beginning of any cattle of that kind in the land." As John Alden and Priscilla had been married more than a year, the picture of Priscilla riding on a snow-white bull, on her wedding day, is an anachronism. The worst hardships of the Pilgrims were now over. With cattle and good crops, there was not to be any more suffering for food. The existence of the colony was assured.

There were still, however, many trials and discouragements before the colonists. The death of John Robinson, their pastor in Leyden, was a heavy sorrow; for they had hoped each year that he would be able to join them. As Elder Brewster was not a clergyman, and hence not able to administer the sacraments of baptism and the Lord's Supper, they felt that they were a flock without a shepherd. The Elder, however, was faithful in "dispensing the gospel;" and none were allowed to suffer for the lack of hearing the Word. "For every Lords day some are appointed to visit suspected places, and if any be found idling, and neglect ye hearing of ye word (through idlnes or profanes,) they are punished for ye same."

There was some internal dissension and hard feeling stirred up by those who came "on their particular." The story of John Oldham and Mr. Lyford, and of the colony's dealings with them, as told by Bradford, is intensely dramatic. But by wisdom of the governor all their plottings were brought to naught. There were also some very unpleasant passages with their ill-conducted neighbors at Merrymount, who persisted in selling rum and firearms to the Indians. This "unruly nest" was at last broken up, and its leader sent to England.

The greatest trial of the colony during its first seven years of existence was its uncomfortable relation with the adventurers who had furnished the capital for the enterprise. There were mutterings and discontent on both sides. Many cargoes of beaver fur and clapboard had been sent back to England. In return they received no supplies, but only constant complaints and reproaches and some very undesirable settlers. In 1627 they succeeded in buying out the entire interest of the adventurers for the sum of eighteen hundred pounds, payable in instalments. They thus became the owners of the land on which they were settled, and were able to make an equitable division of property. Bradford and seven others, who became the bondsmen of the colony, undertook to farm its trade, and to pay the whole indebtedness. By the misconduct of their agent, Allerton, the debt was largely increased, but in time all was paid. They also expended several hundred pounds in bringing others of their number from Leyden. The time had now come when the Pilgrims were no longer alone on the continent. Encouraged by their success, hundreds, even thousands, of Englishmen had crossed the seas to escape persecution. They had neighbors at Salem, Boston, Dorchester, and elsewhere. It was a red-letter day when Governor Bradford travelled to Naumkeag (Salem) to give the little church there organized the right hand of fellowship.

When Bradford had filled the office of governor for twelve years, he succeeded in pressing Winslow into the service for one year. Winslow was succeeded by Prince; but the next year Bradford was again forced into the harness, which he wore, except for three short intermissions, until his death.

It was a sorrowful day for the governor when some of the "Mayflower's" passengers, — notably, Miles Standish, John Alden, and the

Brewsters — took their families across the harbor to found the town of Duxbury. Bradford feared that this division of the church would provoke the Lord's displeasure, and considered an earthquake which occurred about that time a visible sign of such disapproval. But the seceders remained, and others followed their example. By 1640 the colony consisted of eight towns. The duties of the governor were heavier and more complex; but he found time to continue his history, to write a poem now and then, and to begin the study of Hebrew, that he might see with his own eyes something of that holy tongue in which the laws and oracles of God were written. Before leaving Holland he had studied Greek and Latin, French and Dutch. He was also well skilled in history, antiquity, philosophy, and theology, says Cotton Mather. And now in his old age he turned his attention to Hebrew. At the back of his manuscript history are several pages of Hebrew exercises in Bradford's writing, with the following note prefixed: "Though I am growne aged, yet I have had a longing desire to see, with my owne eyes, something of that most ancient language, and holy tongue, in which the Law and oracles of God were write; and in which God, and angels, spake to the holy patriarks of old time; and what names were given to things, from the creation. And though I canot attaine to much herein, yet I am refreshed to have seen some glimpse hereof (as Moyses saw the land of Canan a farr of). My aime and desire is, to see how words and phrases lye in the holy texte; and to discerne somewhat of the same, for my owne contente."

In 1655 Bradford filed eight objections to a re-election; but they were all overruled, and he was chosen governor for the thirtieth time. The following year he was again chosen, with Standish, as usual, for one of the assistants. At the next annual meeting both their seats were vacant. Winslow had died the year before. That noble trio which had served the colony for so many years, the ready tongue, the firm hand, the wise brain, were all at rest. Bradford's body was carried to the top of Burial Hill. No religious services were held; for that would have "savored of Popery." The whole community stood quietly by till the grave was filled and a volley fired over it. The Pilgrims knew what they had lost, and so long as any survivors of the "Mayflower" were left, they loved to speak of Bradford as the "Common blessing and father of us all."

THE EARLY AUTOCRAT OF NEW ENGLAND.

THE EARLY AUTOCRAT OF NEW ENGLAND.

NO people in the world were ever more jealous of ritual and liturgy — the authority of church and priest — than the early settlers of New England. In their fear of a hierarchy they did not allow the clergy to hold certain offices, and they prevented them from officiating at funerals and weddings. The marriage ceremony was performed by magistrates. They disliked the word church, and called the place where they assembled for worship the "meeting-house."

In spite of all this watchful care against the form and letter of the hierarchy, no people were ever more thoroughly under the control of the clergy than these same early settlers of New England. The real autocrat of early New England was the Puritan preacher. And it was not alone from the pulpit that he exercised authority; his hand was seen in every matter, great and small. The laws by which the colony was to be governed were framed by him. True, the code based on Joshua and Jeremiah, drawn up by "that godly, grave, and judicious divine," Mr. John Cotton, was rejected; but the code which was finally adopted — the famous "Body of Liberties" — was framed by another clergyman, — the Rev. Nathaniel Ward, of Ipswich.

So great was the esteem and honor in which the clergy were held that "speaking slanderously or reproachfully of the minister" was an offence to be met with dire punishment. The offender was required to "stand two hours openly upon a block four feet high, on a lecture day, with a paper fixed upon his breast, with the words 'A WANTON GOSPELLER' written in capital letters, that others might fear and be ashamed of breaking out into the like wickedness." A man in Windham was punished for saying he "had rather hear his dog bark than to hear Mr. Bellamy preach," and promised thereafter to put a guard upon his tongue. A New Haven man was whipped for saying he received no profit from the minister's sermons. Mistress Oliver, for "reproaching the elders," was forced to stand in public with a cleft stick on her tongue. In short, in most of the towns, "speaking deridingly of the minister's powers," or "casting uncharitable reflections on the minister," was a crime to be avoided.

In laying out a new town, the first thing to be done was to select a site for a meetinghouse; the second step was setting aside fifty acres for the minister, — "it being as unnatural for a right New England man to live without an able ministry as for a Smith to work his iron without a fire," as Johnson tells us in his "Wonder Working Providence." In the list of things noted in 1629, which were needed for New England, the order is: "first, ministers; second, Patent under Seal; third, Seal;" and after that, seed grains of various sorts. The reason for this ascendency of the clergy is not far to seek. One of the earliest Puritan preachers, the Rev. Francis Higginson, writes: "Let it never be forgotten, that our New England was originally a plantation of religion and not a plantation of trade. And if there be a man among you who counts religion as twelve, and the world as thirteen, let such a one remember that he hath neither the spirit of a true New England man, nor yet of a sincere Christian."

There were few indeed of the early colonists who counted religion as twelve and the world as thirteen. Religion stood first with them. The government which they thought to found was, as one of their number described it, a theocracy. They planned a sort of "Biblical Commonwealth, of which God should be the ruler and the Bible the statute book." They had no thought of founding a democracy. Said Cotton: "Democracy I do not conceyve that ever God did ordeyne as a fitt government eyther for church or commonwealth. If the people be governors, who shall be governed?" They could conceive of no circumstances in which the Bible was not an explicit guide. To quote again from the Rev. John Cotton, who was one of their chief advisers: "I am very apt to believe that the word and Scriptures of God doe conteyne a short *upoluposis*, or platforme, not only of theology, but also of other sacred sciences, attendants, and hand maids therunto, — ethicks, oeconomics, politics, church-government, prophesy, academy. It is very suitable to God's-all-sufficient wisdom, and to the fulness and perfection of Holy Scriptures, not only to prescribe perfect rules for the right ordering of a private man's soule, but also for the right ordering of a man's family, yea, of the commonwealth too. When a commonwealth hath liberty to mould his own frame, I conceyve the Scripture hath given full direction for the right ordering of the same."

For more than ten years they had no other code of law than God's word. And when, in 1641, the "Body of Liberties" was adopted, the preamble provided that "in case of the defect of the law in any particular case, the matter should be decided by the word of God; according to that Word to be judged by the General Court."

Under such a government, and with such a code, who would take a higher position than the men whose main business in life was to expound and explain the word of God and apply it to private life? Moreover, the clergy were the most learned men in the colony, and were well fitted to take part in its councils. They were, without exception, graduates of the universities and men of ability. So it was only natural that in all grave and perplexing cases the pastors of the churches should be called in to counsel and advise with the General Court.

There was no use for lawyers. We find but one lawyer in the colonial history of Boston, and he had a sorry time of it. This was Thomas Lechford, who, in his three years' residence, had but one case, and was all the time regarded with distrust and suspicion by magistrates and people. He returned to England in disgust, and wrote one of the most interesting books on New England, called " Plain Dealing."

Another circumstance which added to the influence of the clergy was the limitation of the franchise. We have said that the colonists were not planning a democracy. They had their distinctions; but the aristocracy which they planned was not to rest upon birth or wealth or conquest, but on the singular requisite of "goodness." Their test of goodness was that men should worship God in the same way that they did; and they therefore settled the question of the franchise very simply, by allowing none to vote who were not members of the church. The motive assigned was, "that the body of the commons may be possessed of good and honest men." We might think it would be easy to join the church for the sake of securing one's political rights; but it was not so simple a matter as it looks to us. The conferring with the church officers, the being propounded, having one's past life examined, and making public rehearsal of one's private experience, made it a complex affair not to be lightly undertaken. There were times when not more than one fifth of the male population of Boston were church members and voters.

But if deprived of the franchise, the non-voters were by no means deprived of church privileges. Indeed, these privileges were thrust upon them. Not only were they governed by the churchly rules, and obliged to help support the pastor, but, whether they would or not, they had to listen to his sermons. If any one absented himself from church, he was hunted up by the tithing-man, and fined five shillings for the first offence. If he stayed away a whole month together, he could be put in the stocks or in the wooden cage. He had to come in time too. In Scituate, one Bryant entered the church after service had begun, and Parson Wetherell, at the close of his prayer, thus addressed him: "Neighbor Bryant, it is to your reproach that you have disturbed the worship by entering late, living as you do within a mile of this place; and especially so since here is Goody Barstow, who has milked seven cows, made a cheese, and walked five miles to the house of God in good season." The New Haven code of laws ordered that profanation of the Lord's Day should be punished by fine, imprisonment, or corporal punishment; "and if proudly, and with a high hand against the authority of God, — *with death.*"

Though it was dangerous to stay away from church, it was still more dangerous to go, unless one were able to place a guard upon one's tongue. We have seen how "Wanton Gospellers" fared; and the old records of the different towns are full of sentences against those whose criticisms were too free. "Nathaniel Haddock was sentenced to be severely whipped for declaring that he could receive no profit from Mr. H.'s preaching. Thomas Maule received ten stripes for declaring that Mr. H. preached nothing but lies, and that his instruction was the doctrine of devils. The wife of Nicholas Phelps was sentenced to pay five pounds or be whipped, for asserting that this same Mr. H. sent abroad his wolves and bloodhounds among the sheep and lambs." Nor was it enough to abstain from criticism. One had to give respectful attention to the sermon; for the tithing-man was on the watch to see that every one kept awake. He had his rod, with a fox-tail on one end and a ball on the other. If it were a woman who fell asleep, her face was brushed with the fox-tail; if a man, he received a smart tap on the head from the ball end. Thomas Scott, of Lynn, was snoring so audibly that a sound rap was necessary to awaken him. He started up angrily, and knocked the officer down. For this offence he was taken to court and condemned to be severely whipped for "common sleeping" at public worship, and for striking him that waked him. Then the boys! It is a relief to find how much akin these Puritan boys were to the boys of to-day. In the records of a justice of the peace in Connecticut are notes of their "rude and idel behavior in the meting hows, such as Smiling and Larfing, and pulling the hair of his nayber, benoni Simkins in the time of public worship." Some churches were obliged to allow twenty shillings a year to an officer for looking to the boys, and keeping peace in the church. It was no small task to sit still and keep awake during a sermon which lasted from two to three hours, and that, too, in a church without heat. Judge Sewall records that on one occasion the sacrament bread was frozen so hard that it rattled in the plate like beads. And still the congregation sat solemnly quiet until the minister got safely through his finally and lastly.

If reverence for the minister was thus rigidly enforced, still more strict were the laws with regard to reverence for the church and all that it stood for. Profanity was one of the worst of crimes. A man in Hartford, for "his filthy and profane expressions, viz. that hee hoped to meet some of the members of the Church in Hell before long, and he did not question but hee should," was committed to prison, "there to be kept in safe custody till the sermon, and then to stand the time thereof in the pillory, and after sermon to be severely whipped." Mr. Tomlin, of Lynn, was fined for saying, "Curse ye woodchuck!" and Mr. Dexter was "putt in ye bilboes for prophane saying dam ye cowe!" What would a Harvard student of to-day say to the case of Thomas Sargeant, a student, two hundred and twenty years ago? "Thomas Sargeant was examined by the Corporation: finally the advice of Mr. Danforth, Mr. Stoughton, Mr. Thatcher, Mr. Mather (then present) was taken. This was his sentence. That being convicted of speaking blasphemous words concerning the H. G.* he should be therefore publickly whipped before all the Scholars. 2. That he should be suspended as to taking his degree of Bachelour (this sentence read to him twice

* The Holy Ghost.

at the P'r'ts, before the committee, and in the Library . . .) 3. Sit alone by himself in the Hall uncovered at meals, during the pleasure of the President and fellows, and be in all things obedient, doing what exercise was appointed him by the President, or else be finally expelled the Colledge. The first was presently put in execution in the Library, . . . before the Scholars. He kneeled down and the instrument Goodman Hely attended to the President's word as to the performance of his part in the work. Prayer was had before and after by the President."* It is safe to say that Thomas did not swear again in college. The prayer before and after the whipping is as characteristic of the times as the sentence itself.

In a community where words were so carefully weighed and morals so closely watched, where the clergy made the laws, and the voters and office-holders had to be

* Sewall's Diary.

church members, we can imagine the influence and prestige of the preacher. There was no talk in that day of keeping politics out of the pulpit. To give his opinion on all public questions, and to inform his people of their duties, was a part of his task. The election sermon was one of the great events of the year. No pastor would neglect to tell his people how to vote. His preaching was not confined to the Sabbath. There was the "great and Thursday," as they called it, — the weekly lecture, which was to the seventeenth century what the opera is to the nineteenth. It was their one dissipation; and it became so much of a dissipation that the General Court had to interfere to regulate the hours. It was held on Thursday in Boston, and on other days in the neighboring towns; and there was much going back and forth on these days. Judge Sewall often took long rides in order to be in Salem or elsewhere on lecture day, which was a day of visiting and hospitality. There were other things besides the Gospel to give zest to the Thursday lecture. On that day the names of those who were intending marriage were called aloud in the church. Those who had committed some misdemeanor were publicly reproved before the whole congregation. Greater offenders were placed, during lecture hour, in the pillory, or the stocks, which stood on either side of the meeting-house. People with troubled consciences sometimes arose during the service and made confession of secret sins. It was also the day for the whipping-post. Therefore there was no knowing what event you might miss if you stayed away from the Thursday lecture.

The life of a minister was not a sinecure. In addition to the Sunday sermons and the Thursday lecture, Mr. Cotton preached three times a week besides, — on Wednesday and Thursday evening and Saturday afternoon.

He also held a daily lecture in his own house. Then there were the fast days and other special days, when he would "spend six hours in the word and in prayer." The Rev. Joshua Moody wrote four thousand sermons in his lifetime. Preaching was only one feature of the pastor's work. Among his other duties were catechising the children of the parish, listening to cases of conscience, giving counsel on every subject, and making pastoral visits. "He must have five or six separate seasons for private prayer daily, devoting each day in the week to special meditations and intercessions — as, Monday to his family, Tuesday to enemies, Wednesday to the churches, Thursday to other societies, Friday to persons afflicted, and Saturday to his own soul."* He must have his fast days both public and private. And as nothing in the world was begun or

* T. W. Higginson, Atlantic Essays, p. 199.

ended without prayer, he must officiate very frequently in that way.

One would think this clerical life was as full as it could be crowded; but in addition to these manifold duties, the pastor often had to earn his own living, either by tilling the acres given him or by skill in some other direction; for his salary was by no means in proportion to his authority. Parson Everett, of Sandwich, added to his slender income by sweeping the meeting-house and taking care of it, for which work he was paid the sum of three dollars a year. The same thrifty parson leased a fulling mill, and spent what leisure he had in cleansing the homespun clothes of his parishioners. Some of the pastors earned small sums by drawing up wills and other legal documents. Some studied medicine, and kept a stock of drugs for sale. The inscription on the grave of Michael Wigglesworth, at Malden, records:

> "Here lyes interd in silent grave below
> Maulden's Physician of Soul and Body too."

Others of the pastors were coopers, carpenters, millers, or cobblers. Many of them who had no trade at command received students into their families to prepare for college.

It might be thought that in a community which was governed by the laws of Moses, which was settled in the wilderness, and removed from the temptations of cities, the pastor would have but little difficulty in keeping his flock in order,—that he would need to preach only doctrinal sermons. There were doctrinal sermons, it is true; for were there not eighty-two "pestilential heresies" to contend against? But there were also many practical sermons. There were, as we have seen, "pnishouse, odious and Squerulous words" to be suppressed; there were the fashions to be preached about,— the wearing of veils, and of "slashed apparel" and of "immoderate great sleeves." And for the men there were sermons against long hair, and later, against the ungodly fashion of periwigs. If you think it is only in our day that people are the slaves of fashion, listen to what the Rev. Nathaniel Ward, of Ipswich, had to say to the women two hundred and forty years ago. He will borrow, he says, "a little of their loosed tongued liberty and misspend a word or two upon their long waisted but short skirted patience. I honor the woman that can honor herself with her attire; a good text always deserves a fair margent but as for a woman who lives but to ape the newest court fashions, I look at her as the very gizzard of a trifle, the product of a quarter of a cipher, the epitome of nothing; fitter to be kicked if she were of a kickable substance than either honored or humored. To speak moderately, I truly confess, it is beyond my understanding to conceive how these women should have any true grace or valuable virtue, that have so little wit as to disfigure themselves with exotic garbs, as not only dismantles their native, lovely lustre but transclouts them into gaunt bar-geese, ill shapen shotten shellfish, Egyptian hieroglyphics, or at the best into French flirts of the pastry, which a proper English woman should scorn with her heels. It is no marvel they wear drails on the hinder part of their heads; having nothing, it seems, in the forepart but a few squirrels' brains to help them frisk from one ill favored fashion to another."

There were also sermons to be preached against the popish superstitions of keeping Christmas and saints' holidays. There were certain worldly practices and amusements that new comers were trying to bring over. If we would see how they handled their subjects, we may read Increase Mather's sermon entitled, "Testimony against several popular and superstitious customs now practiced by some in New England. Against stage plays, promiscuous dancing, health drinking, cards and dice and such like games.

Against profane Christmas keeping. Against New Year's gifts. Candlemas, Shrove Tuesday. The vanity of making cakes on such a day."

As for more serious subjects, we learn from Cotton Mather with what enemies they had to contend. The seventh book of his remarkable Magnalia, entitled "A Book of the Wars of the Lord," narrates the afflictive disturbances which the churches of New England have suffered from their various adversaries, viz.: "the Devil, Separatists, Familists, Antinomians, Quakers, Clerical imposters and Indians." As for the first of these, we fear he is still abroad in the land; and for the last of the seven, — the Indians — they were regarded as the natural children of the devil, his worshippers and followers. To exterminate them was to weaken the powers of darkness. Eliot and Mayhew, indeed, prayed for their conversion; but during King Phillip's War, Increase Mather prayed openly, in the pulpit, every Sunday, for the death of that miserable monarch. On a certain Sunday he forgot to insert that clause in his prayer, and was greatly troubled by the omission, until he learned afterward that his prayers had already been effectual, — that King Phillip had died before the Sunday in question. The other enemies mentioned — Separatists, Familists, Antinomians, and Quakers — were, most of them, conquered after long and bitter struggles, and driven forth into that "Paradise of heretics," — Rhode Island.

Not all of them, however, reached that haven. Some few were put to death. We who love New England may, indeed, wish that no Quakers had ever been hanged on Boston Common. But we may wish also that the Quakers had not chosen to go through the streets and into the churches naked, or clothed in sackcloth and ashes. And we must admit that even our tolerant modern divines would find it somewhat irritating to have people stand up in the congregation and interrupt the sermon with such epithets as these: "Thou firebrand! thou moon-calf! thou gormandizing priest! thou bane of reason and beast of the earth!" We must remember, too, that these disturbers of the peace were begged to leave in peace, and take themselves and their heresy elsewhere; but that they persisted in returning to Boston, and courted death by making themselves as conspicuous as possible. We must remember also that the Quakers were not merely heretics; they opposed themselves to the political order of things. They would not bear arms or pay taxes; they refused allegiance to the charter, and denied the authority of the laws. Moreover, it was not an age of toleration. Those who have said that our Puritan forefathers came here to found freedom of worship, and then turned persecutors themselves, have wholly mistaken their motives. Liberty of worship was farthest from their thoughts. They came here to worship God in their own way; but they were just as certain that their way was *the* way as was ever Archbishop Laud himself. They believed that the presence of such people would endanger the Commonwealth, and that they had a right to brand them with H. for heretic, and R. for rogue, and drive them from their midst. "Let us be just, even to the unjust!" says Colonel Higginson.

In any history of the founders of New England how many of the honored and familiar names belong to the ranks of the clergy! We cannot think of Hartford without Thomas Hooker; of Providence without Roger Williams; of Cambridge without the "holy, heavenly, sweet-affecting, soul-ravishing Mr. Shephard;" or of Boston without John Cotton and the three generations of Mathers, — father, son, and grandson. In the old burying-ground on Copp's Hill is a table-like monument bearing the names of Increase Mather and Cotton Mather. The names on the moss-covered stone are almost illegible, and the memory of them has also grown dim in men's minds; but no two men ever had greater influence in Boston than the two who lie in this forgotten grave.

Historians refer to their day as the Mather dynasty. Increase Mather (whose name "was given him by his father because of the never-to-be-forgotten Increase, of every sort, wherewith God favored the country, about the time of his Nativity,") was for more than sixty years the pastor of the old North Church, and during a great part of that time was also president of Harvard College. From his diaries we might think his whole life was given up to ecstatic prayers, divine afflations, and visions; but he gave the closest attention to public affairs. Although he held no office, no question of importance was decided in Boston without his advice. In those dark days when Charles II. was demanding the surrender of her charter from Massachusetts, the freemen of Boston met together, and invited Increase Mather to give them his views of this "Case of Conscience." He urged them to trust themselves in the hands of God rather than in the hands of men, — that is, to hold on to their charter. At the close of his "pungent speech, many of the Freemen fell into tears; and there was a general acclamation, 'We thank you, Syr. We thank you, Syr.'" The assembly voted against the surrender of the charter without a dissenting voice.

When the charter was annulled by James II., and the hated governor, Sir Edmund Andros, sent over, Mr. Mather opposed with great plainness every encroachment of the new government. Andros and his associates recognized his power, and paid him the compliment of hating him thoroughly. "New

England's Mahomett," they called him, — "The Bellows of Sedition and Treason." When the tyranny of Andros became unendurable, and the colony decided to send an agent to England to complain of it and to labor for a new charter, Mr. Mather was chosen for the mission. He had two or three audiences with King James, and obtained fair promises from the crafty king; but before anything was done, James was obliged to flee, and the power passed into the hands of William and Mary. The new monarchs had so many important problems to solve that they could not, at first, give special thought to the colonies across the sea. Therefore they issued a circular letter to all the colonies, confirming the old governors until further orders. This would reinstate Sir Edmund Andros. But, in the mean time, the people of Boston, as soon as they heard of the revolution in England, had risen up in revolt, had placed Andros and his associates in prison, and had restored the old government as it was under the charter. Increase Mather knew that if Andros were restored to power, though only for a short time, he would bitterly revenge himself for the indignities he had suffered. Mather, therefore, took upon himself the responsibility of interfering with the royal letter, and in some way succeeded in stopping it. He then waited upon the king and queen at every opportunity, and pressed the claims of New England. With all his efforts he could not obtain the restoration of the old charter; and the charter that he finally secured was very unsatisfactory to the colonists. It left to the king the appointment of a governor. There were some advantages, however, which they failed to appreciate. Although the crown appointed the governor, the colonists paid him, and in their own way; and that gave them a hold upon the royal governors which they did not fail to use, down to the time of the Revolution. The king showed his appreciation of Mr. Mather's importance by the singular favor of allowing him to choose the new governor, as well as the other officers to be appointed by the crown. Mr. Mather chose for the first governor that famous knight, Sir William Phipps, whose history is a romance by itself.

The new charter had one provision which was very distasteful, even to Mr. Mather. It extended the franchise to allow other than church members to vote. This, so far as the power of the clergy was concerned, was the "beginning of the end." Increase Mather was the last possessor of the almost absolute power of the Puritan clergy. Nevertheless, for a time, nearly equal power and importance belonged to his son, Cotton Mather, who was descended not only from the Mathers, but from the "father and glory of Boston,"— John Cotton. An epitaph was written for his grandfather, —

"Here lies Richard Mather,
Who had a son greater than his father,
And a grandson greater than either."

We can best understand the spirit of those old Puritan divines, and the atmosphere in which they lived, by a glance at Cotton Mather's childhood. Truly, in his case, the child was father to the man. He began to pray, he says, when he began to speak. He used secret prayer, not confining himself to forms. But when he was seven or eight years old, he composed forms of prayer for his schoolmates and *obliged* them to pray. "I rebuked my playmates for their wicked words and ways; and sometimes suffered from them the persecution of not only Scoffs but Blows also, for my rebukes." His chief fault, he says, was idleness; yet we find that at the age of eleven he could speak Latin so readily that he was able to write the notes of sermons in that language. He had conversed with Cato, Terence, Tully, Ovid, and

Virgil, had made epistles and themes, had gone through a great part of the New Testament in Greek, had read considerably in Socrates and Homer, and had made some entrance into Hebrew grammar. Before he came to the age of fourteen, he had "composed Hebrew exercises and ran through the other sciences." At twelve he was admitted to Harvard College, and graduated at sixteen. When he took his second degree, the subject of his thesis was, "The Hebrew vowel points are of divine origin."

He was but twenty years old when he was called to be his father's assistant in the North Church; and he remained minister of that church all his life. A leaf from his diary gives a glimpse of his daily life at this time. "Read Exodus, 34, 35, 36. Prayed, Examined the children; read Descartes; read commentators; breakfasted; prepared sermon; took part in family prayer; heard pupils recite; read Salmon on medicine; dined;

visited many friends; read various books; prepared sermon; heard pupils recite; meditated; prayed; supped; prepared sermon; took part in family prayer." As the record of a week's work we find that he preached on Lord's Day and on Monday, Tuesday, Wednesday, and Thursday. He very often preached five times in one week, and sometimes five times in two days. In one year he observed sixty private fast days and twenty vigils. On one occasion two friends happened in when he was busy with a private fast, and instead of giving it up, he "preached unto them three sermons, each of them about an hour long apeece." Naturally, with so much fasting and prayer, he saw visions. At one time an angel appeared to him in white and shining robes, with wings and a tiara. He had also his personal encounters with the devil. He records his temptations in Latin, for fear, as he adds in Latin, "lest my dear wife, sometime looking over these papers, should understand it." What wonder then that he believed not only in the bad spirits and the good, but also in demoniacal possession, and was firmly convinced that certain people had sold themselves to the devil, and had become witches! The darkest stain upon the name of Cotton Mather is his relation to the witchcraft tragedy. There are those who still refuse to believe him sincere in that matter, who accuse him of having fomented the excitement in order to restore his own and his father's waning power. But the more we see him as he saw himself, and the more we study his diary, the more we are convinced that, however misguided, he was sincere. There was no question of not believing in witchcraft. Everybody believed in witchcraft. The history of that remarkable craze is another story, and it is only touched upon here because of the obloquy which has attached to Cotton Mather on account of it. Historians have left a terrible picture of him on his white horse, riding around the common, during the hanging of the witches, stirring the people up to greater fury. But there is no doubt that, with his emotional and excitable nature, Cotton Mather felt that he was waging a personal war with Satan for the control of New England.

Of his emotional nature we have many proofs in his diaries. He is always on the mountain-top or in the valley. He is either "under a divine afflatus, wonderfully irradiated," or else he is full of "dejected and abasing thoughts of his own extraordinary vileness." He is frequently prostrate on his study floor, in the dust; and he speaks of leaving floods of tears upon the floor. When preparing a sermon, he says, "I first laid my sinful mouth in the Dust on my Study-floor before the Lord, where I cast myself, in my supplications for His Assistance and Acceptance, as utterly unworthy thereof." It is difficult for us to conceive of the extremely personal character of his religion, — his constant communication with the "invisible world." His relations with the devil were equally personal. One Sunday morning Satan's emissaries stole the carefully prepared notes of his sermon. He entered the pulpit, nevertheless, and preached extempore. "So the divil got nothing out of it," he said. When the demons brought their books for the possessed to sign away their souls, he regarded it as a direct defiance from hell against his efforts; for he worked for God by writing books. After this challenge he worked more busily at it than ever. The titles of his printed works number three hundred and eighty-three, — all of them religious or theological. It was a poor year that did not bring out ten or twelve works from his pen. His great work, his labor of love, was the "Magnalia Christi Americana," or, the "Ecclesiastical History of New England." Considered as literature, the Magnalia is very dull reading; but as a mirror of the Puritan style of thinking, it is invaluable.

We have seen that the new charter, which gave the privilege of voting to non-church members, dealt a heavy blow to the clergy. The witchcraft tragedy finally broke the power of the theocracy. For the last thirty years of their lives, the Mathers — father and son — fought an ever-losing battle against the new order of things. They used every means in their power, both fair and foul, historians say, to restore the polity of the fathers. But all in vain. The theocracy could not be restored. The old régime ended with the Mathers. The ministers of the eighteenth century occupied a very different position from those of the nineteenth. The keys of heaven and hell they might still hold, but the management of the affairs of this world was taken out of their hands. The days of the autocrat were over!

AN OLD-TIME MAGISTRATE.

AN OLD-TIME MAGISTRATE.

THE seventeenth century was fortunate in possessing three of the most princely gossips that ever lived, — Saint Simon in France, the immortal Pepys in England, and the good Judge Sewall in Boston. Each of these men wrote down from day to day, apparently for his own use, the occurrences of the day, — the details of the life about him; and each has given us an incomparable picture of the world in which he lived, — a picture which no historian, biographer, poet, or painter could have equalled. And they have painted three widely differing worlds. Nothing could better illustrate the differences between the countries they represent than the pages of these old diaries of the seventeenth century.

With Saint Simon the world means the Court of France, and the problem of life resolves itself into a question of precedence. The privilege of being present at the *petit lever* and the *petit coucher*, the king's getting up and the king's going to bed, is an honor worth any amount of striving and fighting and fawning. Life has no higher reward than the honor of being chosen to place upon the sacred body of majesty the royal shirt. What conflicts, what heart burnings, what cruel disappointments, what bitter enmities in that long and weary struggle over the all-important question as to which of the peers are entitled to keep their hats on in the king's presence! Saint Simon, it is true, does sometimes take a look at the busy, swarming multitude who live outside the palace of Versailles, but only as a man somewhat interested in natural history might watch with curiosity the habits of the animals which were created for his comfort and support. There is enough of corruption and immorality in the great palace; intrigue and scandal are the daily food of this nobility, so proud of its birth. But it is sin with its dress-coat on, taking itself seriously, which is almost as dull and uninteresting as virtue itself.

In the pages of Pepys we still have something of the Court; but it is no longer the Court of the grand monarch; it is the Court of Charles II. and Nell Gwynne. The subject of life is no longer dignity, but pleasure. Pepys tells us over and over again that he had a "mighty good time," that it was "mighty pleasant," that he and his friends were "mighty merry together." There is plenty of good eating and drinking, and sometimes the cheerful record, "drunk and so to bed." There are actors and actresses, and "drunken, roaring courtiers." There are hundreds of interesting people who have nothing to do with the Court. For Pepys confesses that he hobnobs with "tag, rag, and bobtail," and often spends his nights in dancing, singing, and drinking. When we go to the play, we go behind the scenes and joke and carry on with the actress; and poor Pepys sometimes carries this so far that his wife, in her jealousy, waves the tongs over his head, and threatens a beating. Pepys, in his turn, is jealous, and has been known to give his wife a black eye. But we must not forget that in spite of all this he is a respectable man, occupying a prominent public position. As to his moral standard, he thinks it is not decent to be more honest than those around him. In regard to his taxes, he feels some scruples about cheating, but fears it would "be thought vain glory" if he did differently from the rest. So, rather than appear eccentric, he will remain a thief. He says he will not be bribed to be unjust, but is "not so squeamish as to refuse a present after." There is immorality enough in this world of Pepys; but it wears its every-day clothes, and is vastly more interesting than the stately vice which solemnly parades itself in the pages of Saint Simon.

Turning from these books to the diary of Judge Sewall is like turning away from the footlights, and from the heavy, unnatural atmosphere of the theatre, to come out into the pure air, under a clear sky. For a glimpse of his moral standpoint as compared with theirs, take this incident which the judge records with pain: "September 3d 1686 — Mr. Shrimpton, Captain Lidget and others come in a Coach from Roxbury about nine o'clock or past, singing as they come, being inflamed with Drink. At Justice Morgan's they stop and drink Healths, curse, swear, talk profanely and baudily, to the great disturbance of the Town and grief of good people. Such high handed wickedness has hardly been heard of before in Boston." There we have the worst that can be said of Boston. A few drunken rowdies riding through the streets — an every-day affair in London — is the most high-handed wickedness this Puritan community has ever known.

The diary of Judge Sewall fills four volumes of the Massachusetts Historical Society's collection, and is a storehouse to which the student must always go, if he would understand the New England Puritan of the second generation. The worthy magistrate little dreamed, as he jotted down from day to day the doings of himself, his family, and his neighbors, including their little peculiarities and peccadilloes, that he was bestowing a boon for which posterity would never cease to be grateful.

The author of the diary was Samuel Sewall, a resident of New England for seventy years, and, for a great part of that period, one of her magistrates. His father, Henry Sewall, "out of dislike to the English Hierarchy," came to this country in 1634, and settled in Newbury. He married there; but a little later, when the rule of Cromwell made England more tolerable for the Puritans, he returned to the old home. Samuel was born at Bishop Stoke in 1652. The restoration of the worst of the Stuarts — King Charles II. — brought the family back to New England in 1661, when Samuel was nine years old. After five years' instruction from the Rev. Mr. Parker, the blind preacher of Newbury, he entered Harvard College at the age of fourteen. The college was still very primitive. The tuition was paid in produce; and the government of the students was strictly paternal, corporal punishment being by no means uncommon. Yet they turned out good, solid men. Unfortunately, Sewall's diary does not begin until after his college days. After graduation he became a Resident Fellow of the college, and was keeper of the library. He was strongly inclined to the ministry; and among the first entries of the journal it is frequently set down that he "commonplaced," — *i. e.*, delivered religious discourses to the students. He records also his first sermon, when, "being afraid to look on the glass, he ignorantly and unwittingly stood two hours and a half." He was for some time undecided as to the choice of a profession, and was greatly exercised with regard to his "spiritual estate." But at last he gave up the idea of the ministry, and settled down into a devout and conscientious layman.

We get curious glimpses into the Puritan habit of mind from the pious reflections he was wont to make in connection with the most ordinary and trivial events. When he fed his chickens, he reflected on his own need of spiritual food, and hoped that he should not nauseate daily duties of prayer, etc. When he sat down to a solitary dinner of baked pigeons, he prayed that he might be "wise as a Serpent and as harmless as a

Dove." When he is weighed, he prays that "the Lord may add or take away from our corporal weight, so as shall be most advantageous for our spiritual growth." Feeling, on the Lord's Day, "dull and heavy and listless as to spiritual Good; Carnal, Lifeless;" he sighed to God that he would quicken him. The next day, when his house is broken into and twenty pounds' worth of silver and linen stolen, he regards it as an answer to his prayer, because he was helped to submit to the stroke. When the thief is caught and put in prison, "the stroke is turned into a kiss of God."

In $167\frac{5}{6}$ Sewall was married to Hannah Hull, daughter of Capt. John Hull of pine-tree shilling fame. Mistress Hannah had been present at Harvard when the young student took his degree, and had set her affections on him at that time, although he knew nothing of it until after their marriage, two years later. The diary makes no mention of the marriage; but tradition tells us that the bride was valued as worth her weight in silver, and that the carefully weighed amount went with her as her dowry. Many times was the husband called upon to stand in the Old South Church and offer up to God in baptism a tiny morsel of humanity. Some of these children died in infancy; but others always came to take their places, "so that by the underserved goodness of God," says the father, "we were never without a child." Fourteen children were born from this marriage; and scattered through the pages of the diary are quaint pictures of the solemn life of the staid little Puritans. The father sadly records: "November 6, 1692. Joseph threw a knop of brass and hit his Sister Betty on the forhead so as to make it bleed and swell; upon which, and for his playing at Prayer-time, and eating when Return Thanks, I whipd him pretty smartly. When I first went in (call'd by his Grandmother) he sought to shadow and hide himself from me behind the head of the Cradle: which gave me the sorrowfull remembrance of Adam's carriage." Joseph, at this time, when he committed the sin of eating when thanks was being returned, and playing in prayer time, was four years old.

Poor little Betty's troubles, however, were the worst. How one's heart aches for the poor little tortured soul! Betty's troubles began when she was only eight years old, when it fell to her share to read in family prayer the twenty-fourth chapter of Isaiah with its dread pictures of the judgments of God. Betty read with many tears; and the contents of the chapter, and sympathy with her, drew tears from the father also. When Betty was about fifteen, Judge Sewall came home one night to find the family in distress. "She had given some signs of dejection and sorrow; but a little after diner she burst out into an amazing cry, which caused all the family to cry too; Her Mother asked the reason; she gave none; at last she said she was afraid she should goe to Hell, her sins were not pardon'd. She was first wounded by my reading a Sermon of Mr. Norton's about the 5th of Jan. Text Jno. 7.34. Ye shall seek me and shall not find me. And those words in the Sermon Jno. 8.21. Ye shall seek me and shall die in your sins, ran in her mind, and terrified her greatly. And staying at home Jan. 12 she read out of Mr. Cotton Mather—Why hath Satan filled thy heart, which increas'd her Fear. Her Mother ask'd her whether she pray'd. She answer'd Yes; but feared her prayers were not heard because her Sins not pardon'd." The pastor was sent for and "pray'd excellently, but without effect."

For a whole week the child had been carrying this dreadful fear before she spoke of it. A few weeks later the father writes: "Feb. 22, 169$\frac{5}{6}$— Betty comes in to me almost as soon as I was up and tells me the disquiet she had when waked; told me was afraid should go to Hell, was like Spira, not Elected. Ask'd her what I should pray for, she said, that God would pardon her Sin and give her a new heart. I answer'd her Fears as well as I could, and pray'd with many Tears on either part; hope God heard us. I gave her solemnly to God." Two months later he records: "Betty can hardly read her chapter from weeping; tells me she is afraid she is gon back, does not taste that sweetness in reading the Word which once she did; fears that what was once upon her is worn off. I said what I could to her and in the evening pray'd with her alone." Betty's fears were never entirely allayed. This terrible shadow of non-election darkened her life even after she was married and had children of her own. On the day of her death her father wrote sadly: "I hope God has delivered her now from all her fears."

Little Sam also had his doubts and fears. He was ten years old when a playmate died of small-pox. The judge thought he ought to " tell Sam. of it and what need he had to prepare for Death, and therefore to endeavor really to pray when he said over the Lord's Prayer: He seemed not much to mind, eating an Aple; but when he came to say, Our father, he burst out into a bitter Cry, and when I ask't what was the matter and he could speak, he burst out into a bitter Cry and said he was afraid he should die. I pray'd with him, and read Scriptures comforting against death, as, O death where is thy sting etc. All things yours, Life and Immortality brought to light by Christ etc." Perhaps Sam's fears were heightened by the fact that his father had, not long before, corrected him for breach of the ninth commandment,— for saying he had been at the writing school when he had not.

Sewall had the greatest confidence in his

wife, as is shown by an entry made in the journal many years after his marriage, — "Jan. 24, 170¾. . . . Took 24 s. in my pocket, and gave my Wife the rest of my cash £4 3-8, and tell her she shall now keep the Cash; If I want I will borrow of her. She has a better faculty than I at managing Affairs: I will assist her; and will endeavor to live upon my Salary; will see what it will doe. The Lord give his Blessing."

Sewall held many public offices after he gave up the ministry. In 1678 he was one of the perambulators of bounds for Muddy River. In 1681 he was appointed to undertake the management of the printing press in Boston. He was one of a committee to draw up instructions for the deputies. In 1683 he was chosen one of the seven commissioners of the town to assess rates. In the same year he became a member of the General Court, — *i. e.*, a deputy. Later he was made a magistrate.

His first years in office were the darkest years in New England. He had but just been made deputy when the king, Charles II., demanded the return of the charter from the colony. "A great town meeting was held in the old South Meeting House, and the moderator requested all who were for surrendering the charter to hold up their hands. Not a hand was lifted, and out from the throng a solitary voice exclaimed, with deep drawn breath, 'The Lord be praised!' Then arose Increase Mather, president of Harvard College, and reminded them how their fathers did win this charter, and should they deliver it up into the spoiler who demanded it even as Ahab required Naboth's vineyard, Oh! their children would be bound to curse them." When the news of this meeting reached London, the charter of the colony was at once annulled. The loss of their charter meant much to these men of Massachusetts. It meant not only that they could no longer elect one of their own number as governor, but that they must be ruled by whomsoever the king would send over; it meant not only that the foundations were taken away on which all their institutions, political and ecclesiastical, rested; it meant also that all their lands reverted to the crown; that the land titles of individuals, which had rested on the charter, were void; that the owners could no longer hold their lands except by paying quit rent to the king.

There is little of definite history in Sewall's record, but there is much insight into the strained relations existing between the new governor, Andros, and the people. One cause of ill will was his appropriating the Old South Meeting-House for the service of the Church of England. He enjoyed the joke of prolonging his services, and keeping the humiliated Puritans outside for an hour or two in the cold, awaiting their turn. This dispute finally led to the building of King's

Chapel, — the first Episcopal church in New England.

During the rule of Andros, Sewall made a journey to London, not only to look after property there, but to join with Increase Mather and others of the colony who were there, in the effort to obtain a restoration of the charter. It was characteristic that before sailing he invited his friends to hold a day of prayer at his home. "Mr. Williard pray'd and preached excellently from Ps. 143. 10; pray'd. Intermission. Mr. Allen pray'd, then Mr. Moodey, both very well, then 3d-7th verses of the 86th Ps., sung Cambridge short Tune, which I set." On his return he again invited in his friends, to the number of twenty, for a service of gratitude. "Mr. Cotton Mather returned Thanks in an excellent maner. Sung part of the Six and fifteth Psalm. I set it to Windsor Tune."

Just as Sewall arrived in England, he was met by the report of the flight of James II.

and the landing of William and Mary. When the news reached Boston, there was great rejoicing. Bells were rung; guns were fired; the citizens came together and clapped the obnoxious governor into prison. They chose old Simon Bradstreet, then eighty-seven years of age, to be their governor once more. They hoped for a restoration of the charter. But William and Mary, though favorably disposed toward Massachusetts, were resolved to govern it in their own way. The new charter was very different from the old. The governors were to be appointed by the crown, instead of elected by the people. All laws passed by the legislature were to be sent to England for royal approval; and the franchise was not to be limited to church members. Massachusetts was no longer a colony. She had become a royal province.

Judge Sewall returned to Boston, and held office under the new régime as he had under the old. He had grave and troublous problems to study. It was the time of the terrible witchcraft excitement. The idea that certain people had sold themselves to the devil and were tormenting their neighbors had taken firm hold of the public mind. A hundred persons were in jail, accused of witchcraft. The governor, Sir William Phipps, appointed a special commission, consisting of seven men, to try these cases. Judge Sewall was one of the seven. By their decision twenty innocent people were put to death. Then came the reaction. The eyes of magistrates and people were opened. They saw their mistake. A day was appointed for fasting and prayer, on account of what might have been done amiss "in the late tragedy, raised among us by Satan and his instruments, through the awful judgment of God." When sickness and death came into Judge Sewall's family, he looked upon it as a direct punishment for his own part in this miserable matter. He winced when Sam, reciting his Latin Scripture les-

AN OLD-TIME MAGISTRATE. 149

son, came to this verse: "If ye had known what this meaneth, I will have mercy and not sacrifice, ye would not have condemned the guiltless." It "did awfully bring to mind the Salem Tragedie," he says. He "put up a bill" for public prayers. There is no more impressive and solemn moment in the life of Judge Sewall than that when he stood up in the South Meeting-House, and listened with bowed head to his own public confession read as follows: "Samuel Sewall, sensible of the reiterated strokes of God upon himself and family; and being sensible, that as to the Guilt contracted upon the opening of the late Commission of Oyer and Terminer at Salem (to which the order for this Day relates) he is, upon many accounts, more concerned than any that he knows of, Desires to take the Blame and shame of it, Asking pardon of men, And especially desiring prayers that God, who has an Unlimited Authority, would pardon that sin and all other his sins; personal and Relative: And according to his infinite Benignity and Sovereignty, Not Visit the sin of him, or of any other, upon himself or any of his, nor upon the Land: But that He would powerfully defend him against all Temptations to Sin, for the future; and vouchsafe him the efficacious, saving Conduct of his Word and Spirit."

None of Sewall's associates in the unhappy business followed his example in doing penance publicly. When the chief judge of the witch trials, Lieutenant-Governor Stoughton, heard of it, he said he had no such confession to make, as he had acted according to the best light God had given him.

Sewall's repentance did not end with this public confession and humiliation. Tradition tells us that every year, for forty years, he set aside a day for prayer and fasting, in remembrance of this greatest mistake of his life. Whittier has preserved this tradition in his beautiful ballad: —

"Touching and sad, a tale is told,
Like a penitent hymn of the Psalmist old,
Of the fast which the good man lifelong kept
With a haunting sorrow that never slept.

. . . . . .

All the day long from dawn to dawn,
His door was bolted, his curtain drawn;
No foot on his silent threshold trod,
No eye looked on him save that of God,
As he baffled the ghosts of the dead with charms
Of penitent tears, and prayers, and psalms,
And, with precious proofs from the sacred word
Of the boundless pity and love of the Lord,
His faith confirmed and his trust renewed
That the sin of his ignorance, sorely rued,
Might be washed away in the mingled flood
Of his human sorrow and Christ's dear blood!"

Whether he kept this anniversary or not, fasts were not infrequent with Judge Sewall. Public fasts were appointed, and these he religiously kept. He was often invited to the houses of his friends to observe a fast with them, and he frequently entertained them in the same way. In addition he had his own private fasts. When affliction visited him, when he had some question to decide, or when he was about to engage in some undertaking on which he desired the blessing of the Lord, he spent a day in prayer and fasting. This was not done for the approval of others. The only account of it is in his diary, written for his eyes alone. None but his family knew when he withdrew into his own room, closed the curtains, shut out the world, and spent the long day in communion with his God.

In his quaint, methodical way he sometimes entered in his journal a list of the subjects which he presented to the Lord in prayer. "February 9; $170\frac{7}{8}$ The Apointment of a Judge for the Super. Court being to be made upon next Fifth day, Febr. 12, I pray'd God to Accept me in keeping a privat day of Prayer with fasting for That and other Important Matters: I kept it upon the Third day Febr. 10, $170\frac{7}{8}$ in the uper Chamber at the North East end of the House, fastening the Shutters next the

Street.—Perfect what is lacking in my Faith and in the faith of my dear Yoke-fellow. Convert my children; especially Samuel and Hanah; Provide rest and Settlement for Hanah: Recover Mary, Save Judith, Elisabeth and Joseph; Requite the Labour of Love of my Kinswoman Jane Tappin, Give her health, find out Rest for her. Make David a man after thy own heart, Let Susan live and be baptised with the Holy Ghost, and with fire. Relations. Steer the Government in this difficult time, when the Governour and many others are at so much Variance: Direct, incline, overrule on the Council-day fifth day, Febr. 12, as to the special Work of it in filling the Super. Court with Justices; or any other thing of like nature; as Plim⁰ infer Court. Bless the Company for propagation of the Gospel, especially Govr Ashurst &c. Revive the Business of Religion at Natick, and accept and bless John Neesnumin who went thither last week for that end. Mr. Rawson at Nantucket. Bless the South Church in preserving and spiriting our Pastor; in directing unto suitable Supply, and making the Church unanimous: Save the Town, College; Province from Invasion of Enemies, open, Secret, and from false Brethern: Defend the Purity of Worship. Save Connecticut, bless their new Governour: Save the Reformation under N. York Governm^t. Reform all the European Plantations in America; Spanish, Portuguese, English, French, Dutch; Save this New World, that where Sin hath abounded, Grace may Superabound; that CHRIST who is stronger, would bind the strong man and spoil his house; and order the Word to be given, Babylon is fallen.—Save our Queen, lengthen out her Life and Reign. Save France, make the Proud helper stoop (Job IX 13), Save all Europe; Save Asia, Africa, Europe and America. These were gen'l heads of my Meditation and prayer;

and through the bounteous Grace of GOD, I had a very Comfortable day of it." The prayer of the Puritan has been compared to the newspaper of to-day. It left out nothing. The atmosphere of prayer is constantly present throughout his life. "There was no variance or break, no stagnation or ebb in his religious life. This was continuous and uniform, in his closet, his family circle, the church, the court room, in college business, the council chamber, the town meeting and the school visitation."

He dwelt upon the thought that in the midst of life we are in death. The subject of death was never far distant from his thoughts. Tombs and graves had a fascination for him. He tells that in visiting the family tomb he was "entertained" by the coffins of his "Father and Mother Hull," and of his six children. He says, "Twas an awful yet pleasing treat." His greatest dissipation was funerals. As we follow the long procession of dead Bostonians whom he helped to lay away, we almost get the impression that he was a professional mourner. He was in great demand as a "Bearer," and found a dignified pleasure in leading the solemn funeral processions through the crooked Boston streets. He carefully records, each time, whether he let down the head or the feet into the grave. He usually had some kind word to say of the departed; but of one poor wight he records that "he lived undesired and died unlamented."

These funerals had their perquisites. It was customary to send gloves to all who were to attend, and "scarves" or rings (sometimes both) to the bearers. The number of scarves, rings, and gloves set down in Sewall's diary would foot up an enormous total. It is related of Dr. Samuel Buxton, of Salem, who died at the age of eighty-one, that he left to his heirs "a quart tankard full of mourning rings which he had received at funerals." One would think Judge Sewall's heirs must have at least a bucket full of these relics. And of gloves and scarves he must certainly have left barrels, unless, like the Rev. Andrew Eliot, he disposed of them in his lifetime. This prudent clergyman received, in thirty-two years, from funerals, weddings, and christenings, two thousand nine hundred and forty pairs of gloves. As he and his family could not wear them all, he sold them through the Boston milliners, and received therefor between six and seven hundred dollars. The quality of the gloves was proportioned to the rank of the wearer.

We are not to think that there were no diversions except funerals. There was feasting as well as fasting, rejoicing as well as mourning. There was plenty of good eating and drinking. We can almost smell and taste the savory food on the Sewall table. The days of short commons among the Puritans were over. After the birth of her fourteenth child Madam Sewall gave a dinner to the various professional nurses whom she had had occasion to employ in past years, to the number of seventeen. It was a gathering one would like to have seen. " Had a good Dinner, Boil'd Pork, Beef, Fowls; very good Rost Beef, Turkey-Pye, Tarts."

Although feasting, fasting, and funerals occupy so large a place in the judge's journal, they were not the serious occupation of his life. He had many duties, and held many positions of trust. He was deputy-councillor, judge, selectman, moderator, overseer of the poor, commissioner of the Society for Propagating the Gospel among the Indians, and Captain of the Ancient and Honorable Artillery Company. In 1699 he was made Judge of the Superior Court; in 1717, Judge of Probate, and in 1718, Chief-Justice.

The office of judge was not a sinecure. It involved holding court in Cambridge, Plymouth, Dedham, Salem, and other towns, in all kinds of weather. It involved frequent journeys, usually on horseback, — journeys that were difficult, uncomfortable, and often dangerous. They had to travel "on rough roads, across ferries, often of icy waters, over marshes and inner seas." He often mentions that in crossing a stream his horse fell under him; and more than one party travelling from Cambridge or Charlestown to Boston barely escaped drowning. The court itself was a solemn affair. There were grave and weighty decisions to be made. Sins of Sabbath breaking, lying, and drunkenness had to be punished. After a disturbance in North's tavern, Mr. Thomas Banister, Jr., is fined "20 shillings for Lying; 5 shillings for Curse, 10s. Breach of the peace for throwing the pots and scale-box at the maid and was bound to his good behavior till next sessions." When an offender was sentenced to prison or to the stocks, pillory, or whipping-post, he was gravely admonished and reproved by the judges. A "woman that had whip'd a man" was sentenced to be whipped; and Judge Sewall informed her that a "woman that had lost her modesty, was like Salt that had lost its savor; good for nothing but to be cast to the Dunghill."

The unlucky wights who sought to introduce dancing into the colony were rigidly suppressed. "Mr. Francis Stepney, the Dancing Master, desired a Jury, so he and Mr. Shrimpton Bound in £50 to January Court. Said Stepney is ordered not to keep a Dancing School; if he does will be taken in contempt and be proceeded with accordingly." A man who was "Setting a room in his House for a man to shew Tricks in" was dealt with in a different manner. The magistrates went to his house, prayed with him, expostulated with him, and sang the ninetieth psalm from the twelfth verse to the end. The treatment seems to have been effectual. The coming of the royal governors and the royal officers and soldiers of their train had brought into the sober Puritan town habits and customs it had never known before; and the judges jealously watched these encroachments, and passed severe sentence against them when possible.

They had also other and graver sins to deal with. Since there were ten crimes that were capital in Massachusetts, sometimes the death sentence had to be passed. A hanging was an affair of the greatest interest. As much publicity as possible was given it for the sake of example. On the Sunday or the lecture-day before the execution the condemned person was brought in chains to the church, and seated in a conspicuous place, to listen to a sermon on his crime. No one failed to be at church on that day; and these improving discourses were printed and sold in great numbers. The whole community made it a point to be in at the death. Even a kindly man like Judge Sewall never stayed away from a hanging.

We have related Sewall's weakness in regard to the subject of witchcraft. We must not fail to credit him with being ahead of his age on three other questions which are still of the greatest interest to us, — the slavery question, the Indian question, and the woman question. Slavery still existed in New England; and to Sewall belongs the honor of publishing the first anti-slavery tract in America. It was entitled, "The Selling of Joseph;" and in it he prays for the rights of the black man, and answers all the arguments in favor of slavery. On the Indian question he also took advanced ground, and labored faithfully and earnestly all his life long for the education of this unfortunate race. On the woman question he wrote the treatise called "Talitha Cumi," in which he pleads for women as joint heirs of the heavenly mansions, and argues learnedly that women will undoubtedly be found in heaven.

Among other books that Sewall wrote there were two on America, in the second of which he considers it scripturally as the future earthly paradise. He spent many years of loving labor on the two bulky volumes with the appalling title of "Phenomena Quaedam Apocalyptica," which deal with the fulfilment of prophecies. Nor did he disdain verse. He sometimes records the making of a couplet as he lies in bed in the morning. Here is one of these morning productions: —

"To Horses, Swine, Net-Cattell, Sheep and Deer,
Ninety and Seven prov'd a Mortal yeer."

A fair sample of his poetry is this hymn on the opening of the new century, which he had the bellman recite through the town on New Year's Day: —

"Once more! our God vouchsafe to shine:
Correct the Coldness of our Clime.
Make haste with thy Impartial Light,
And terminate this long dark night.

> "Give the poor Indians Eyes to see
> The Light of Life: and set them free.
> So Men shall God in Christ adore,
> And worship Idols vain, no more.

> "So Asia, and Africa,
> Europa, with America;
> All Four, in Consort join'd shall Sing
> New Songs of Praise to Christ our King."

On the occasion of a funeral at which two other bearers had the name of Samuel, two were called John, and one Thomas, Sewall made the following couplet, and esteemed it worthy of record: —

> "Three Sams, two Johns, and one good Tom
> Bore Prudent Mary to her Tomb."

The judge was a musician as well as a poet, and for twenty-four years he "set the tunes" in the Old South Church. He led them triumphantly through the "Bay Psalm Book" many times in course; and when he set the psalm well, he recorded the fact with pride. In one respect he was a model for modern musicians. When his musical talent began to fail him, he was the first to notice it. When he intended Windsor and fell into High Dutch, and then, essaying to set another tune, went into a key much too high, he said, "The Lord humble me and instruct me that I should be the occasion of any interruption in the worship of God." When it happened that twice within three weeks he set York Tune, and the congregation carried it over into Saint David's, he took it as a sign that he ought to resign the precentor's place. "I have through the divine Long-suffering and Favour done it for 24. years, and now God by his Providence seems to call me off; my voice being enfeebled." He persisted in giving up this pleasant task, though urged to continue.

Of the judge's genial and kindly side we have many glimpses. His pockets seem to have been always filled with sermons, trinkets, fruits, and goodies. He scarcely ever made a call without leaving behind him a box of "Chocolatt, Marmalad or Figgs," accompanied by a tract. He records in one day the giving away of the "Jews in Berlin," "God's All-Sufficiency," "Cooper's Sermons," "Vincent's Catechism," and forty shillings. Cotton Mather's sermons he sowed broadcast among his friends.

The judge was also stubbornly conscientious, and in following his line of duty often ran counter to the opinions of others and incurred their ill-will. The Rev. Cotton Mather rushed upon him one day in a public place, and declared in a loud voice that he had used his father worse than a "neger." On the next page of the journal we find the entry: "Sent Mr. Increase Mather a haunch of Venison. In that I hope I did not treat him as a negro." His pastor, the Rev. Mr. Pemberton, became offended at Sewall and the rest of the judges, and in church gave out the first five verses of the fifty-eighth psalm to be sung: —

"Speak, O ye judges of the Earth if just your Sentence be:
Or must not Innocence appeal to Heaven from your Decree?

"Your wicked hearts and Judgements are alike by malice sway'd;
Your griping Hands, by weighty Bribes, to Violence betrayed."

Sewall writes in his diary: "I think if I had been in his place and had been kindly and tenderly affectioned, I should not have done it at this time. Another Psalm might have suited his Subject as well."

There was one subject, however, upon which Sewall could not be charitable; this was the wearing of periwigs. He fought a life-long battle against this ungodly fashion which was creeping into New England. When we come upon the entry, "This day I wore my black skull cap in meeting," it seems an unimportant act, but it was in reality a manifesto. His hair was getting thin; and when all the heads about him were covered with flowing periwigs, he covered his with a black skull-cap, which he wore until his death. When any of his friends adopted the obnoxious fashion, he remonstrated with them earnestly. "Mention the words of our Saviour, Can ye not make one hair white or black." He records with almost cruel satisfaction the miserable death of a wigmaker. When Josiah Williard appeared in a wig, Sewall went to him and labored with him. "I enquired of him what Extremity had forced him to put off his own hair and put on a Wigg? He answered none at all. But said that his Hair was streight and that it parted behinde. Seem'd to argue that men might as well shave their hair off their head, as off their face. I answered men were men before they had hair on their faces, (half of mankind have never any). God seems to have ordain'd our Hair as a Test, to see whether we can bring our minds to be content to be at his finding: or whether we would be our own Carvers, Lords, and come no more at Him." Josiah promised to leave off his wig when his hair was grown, but he seems to have forgotten his promise, for he was still wearing it six months later; and when he was to preach in the Old South, Sewall absented himself and attended another church rather than see the hated wig in the pulpit. In summing up the character of a man who had died, he says: "A rare instance of Piety, Health, Strength, Serviceableness. The Wellfare of the Province was much upon his Spirit. He abominated Perriwigs."

We can imagine the judge's feelings when the Rev. Cotton Mather preached a sermon in defence of periwigs. "Said one sign of a hypocrit was for a man to strain at a Gnat and swallow a Camel. Sign in 's Throat discovered him; To be zealous against an inocent fashion taken up and used by the best of men; and yet make no conscience of being guilty of great Immoralities. . . . I expected not to hear a vindication of Perriwiggs in Boston Pulpit by Mr. Mather; however, not from that Text. The Lord give me a good Heart and help to know, and not only to know but also to doe his Will; that my Heart and Head may be his." The senseless fashion, however, continually gained ground, and Sewall was left almost alone in his opposition.

In 1717, after forty-four years of married life, Sewall lost his wife. She had proved herself to be worth far more than her weight in silver to him, and her husband mourned her sincerely.

It was not to be expected, however, that he would remain single. Although he was sixty-six years old, his friends began at once to look about to find a suitable match for him. In a few weeks he himself began to "take notice" of the various widows about him. The elder Mr. Weller had not yet given his famous advice to "bevare of vidders;" nor would it have been of any use in that community. "Godly old maids," like Mary Carpenter, were a rare commodity. It was widows or nothing. Boston had not yet become what Theodore Parker called it later, the "Paradise of old Maids." Sewall began to note the comings and goings of Madam Katherine Winthrop, whose husband had died soon after Mrs. Sewall. It is just four months after the death of his wife that we find the entry in the diary, February 6, "This morning wandering in my mind whether to live a Single or a Married Life." He had already sent Madam Winthrop "Smoking Flax inflamed, the Jewish children of Berlin, and my small vial of Tears." All of his friends approved his choice, and things seemed to be going well, when suddenly his friend, Mr. Denison, died, and the judge turned his eyes to the Widow Denison. To tell the truth, he accompanied her home from the funeral, and prayed God to keep house with the widow. She came to his house to prove the will, and he gave her a "Widows Book Bound, having writ her Name in it." On her next visit he took her up into his chamber, and "discoursed thorowly with her; . . . told her I intended to visit her at her own house next Lecture day. She said, twoul'd be talk'd of. I answered, In such Cases, persons must run the Gantlet." On next lecture-day he kept his word. He gave her Dr. Mather's sermons bound, and she gave him very good curds. On his next visit she invited him to eat. He gave her "two Cases with a knife and fork in each; one Turtle shell tackling; the other long with Ivory handles, Squar'd, cost 4*s.* 6*d.*; Pound of Raisins with proportionable Almonds." Later he gave her a Psalm-book bound with leather, and a pair of shoe-buckles; cost 5*s.* 3*d.* At last he told her he thought it was time to finish the business. But when they came to the very delicate question of settlements, they could not agree. Mr. Denison had left his widow very well to do, and she thought it hard to " give up a certainty for an uncertainty." The more they discussed the subject, the less they agreed. Neither would yield; and the judge wrote, " My bowels yern towards Mrs. Denison, but I think God directs me in his providence to desist." She came once more to see him, on foot from Roxbury, on a cold night, to try to patch the matter up; but no result was reached. She offered to give back his presents, but the elderly lover bade her keep them, " only now they had not the same signification as before. She went away in the bitter Cold, no Moon being up, to my great pain. I Saluted her at parting."

He next visited Mrs. Elizabeth Tilly; and here is the record of one week, in the diary: —

SEPTEMBER 16, After the Meeting I visited Mrs. Tilly.

SEPTEMBER 18, ditto.

SEPTEMBER 21, I gave Mrs. Tilly a little booke entitled "Ornaments for the daughters of Sion." I gave it to my dear Wife August 28 1702.

SEPTEMBER 23, 24, eat Almonds and Reasons with Mrs. Tilly and Mrs. Armitage; Discoursed with Mrs. Armitage, who spake very agreeably, and said Mrs. Tilly had been a great Blessing to them hop'd God would make her so to me and my family.

SEPTEMBER 25, Visited Mrs. Tilly.

The matter was soon settled. Two weeks later the banns were published, and in another two weeks they were married. Sewall's son, the Reverend Joseph, who was the apple of his eye, performed the ceremony "in the best room below stairs. Mr. Prince pray'd the 2^d time. Mr. Adams the Minister of Newington was there, Mr. Oliver and Mr. Tim^o Clark Justices, and many more. Sung the 12, 13, 14, 15, and 16, verses of the 90th Psalm. Cous. S Sewall set Low-dutch Tune in a very good Key, which made the Singing with a good number of Voices very agreeable. Distributed Cake." The next day the governor and his lady, the ex-governor, councillors, and ministers in town, with their wives, dined with them.

The judge's happiness was of short duration. Mrs. Tilly lived but half a year after she had become Mrs. Sewall, and it was all to do over again. He remembered with sadness Madam Winthrop, whom he had left for Mrs. Denison. After a suitable time — three months — he sent his daughter to acquaint Madam Winthrop that if she pleased to be within at three P.M. he would wait upon her. He approaches her this time with great delicacy. "My loving wife died so soon and so suddenly, 't was hardly convenient for me to think of Marrying again; however I came to this Resolution, that I would not make my Court to any person without first Consulting with her." They then discoursed pleasantly about the seven single persons who sat in the fore-seat the previous Sunday. The next day they continued this discourse; and, as she recommended one widow after another, he prayed that Katherine herself might be the one. But she refused, "as if she had catched at an opportunity to do it." The wooer refused to be discouraged, gave her the "Fountain Opened," and said he would call that day Sennight, the 10th. Instead of waiting for the appointed day, however, he called twice within the week; gave her "a piece of Cake and Ginger Bread wrapped up in a clean sheet of Paper;" told her of his loneliness, and that they might help to forward one another in their journey to Canaan. On the 10th he called, and was "treated with a great deal of Curtesy; Wine, Marmalade." On the 11th he sent her the following letter:

MADAM, — These wait on you with Mr. Mayhew's Sermon, and Account of the state of the Indians on Martha's Vinyard. I thank you for your Unmerited Favors of yesterday; and hope to have the Hapiness of Waiting on you tomorrow before Eight aclock after Noon. I pray God to keep you, and give you a joyfull entrance upon the Two Hundred and twenty ninth year of Christopher Columbus his Discovery; and take Leave who am, Madam your humble Servt.

S. S.

When he called next day, he found her full of work behind a stand, and her countenance much changed, — "looked dark and lowering." He got his chair in place, and "had some Converse, but very Cold and indifferent to what 'twas before. Ask'd her to acquit me of Rudeness If I drew off her Glove. Enquiring the reason, I told her 'twas great odds between handling a dead Goat, and a living Lady. Got it off." She, however, persisted in her refusal, recommended other widows to him, and finally twitted him with leaving her for Mrs. Denison. Upon which he told her that if after a first and second vagary she would accept of him returning, " Her Victorious Kindness and Good Will would be very Obliging." He gave her another book. She filled a glass of wine, and sent her servant home with him with a good lantern. "Told her the reason why I came every other night was lest I should drink too deep draughts of Pleasure. She had talked of Canary, her Kisses were to me better than the best Canary." When they came to the question of settlements, Madam Winthrop mentioned her desire that he should keep a coach, and also added the condition that he should wear a wig. The next day his son, the minister, came to him by appointment, and they went into his chamber and prayed together concerning the courtship. Not to much avail, it would seem, for Madam proved cold that night. She offered him no wine; when he rose to go did not offer to help him put on his coat; would not send her servant to light him home, but let him stumble along as best he could. He explained that he could not afford to keep a coach. "As to a Perriwig, My best and greatest Friend, began to find me with Hair before I was born, and had continued to do so ever since; and I could not find in my heart to go to another." The son again came and prayed with his father about the courtship, but with no better success than before.

Mrs. Winthrop was rocking her granddaughter's cradle when he came, and she placed the cradle between his chair and hers. "The Fire was come to one short Brand beside the Block;" and when it fell to pieces and she did not replenish it, he took the hint. "Took leave of her . . . did not bid her draw off her Glove as sometime I had done. Her Dress was not so clean as sometime it had been. Jehovah Jireh!" Thus ended another dream.

The Widow Ruggles proved equally obdurate. "She express'd her inability to be Servicable." She even "made some Difficulty to accept an Election Sermon, lest it should be an obligation on her."

The judge's next attempt was a letter to Mrs. Mary Gibbs, widow, of Newtown: —

JANUARY 12, 17⅔¹.

MADAM,—Your Removal out of Town and the Severity of the Winter, are the reason of my making you this Epistolary Visit. In times past (as I remember) you were minded that I should marry you, by giving you to your desirable Bridegroom. Some sense of this intended Respect abides with me still; and puts me upon enquiring whether you be willing that I should Marry you now, by becoming your Husband; Aged, and feeble, and exhausted as I am, your favorable Answer to this Enquirey, in a few Lines, the Candor of it will much oblige, Madam, your humble Serv't. S. S.

The widow's answer was favorable, and he rode to Newtown in a coach to visit her. Carried her a pound of glazed almonds and "a Duz. Meers Cakes; Two bottles of Canary,"—not such expensive presents as he had given the others; perhaps Mrs. Gibbs was too easily won. They discussed settlements, and she thought him hard. After a good deal of higgling the matter was settled, and the banns were published, upon which he writes to her: "Madam, Possibly you have heard of our Publishment last Thorsday, before now. It remains for us to join together in fervent Prayers, without ceasing, that God would graciously Crown our Espousals with his Blessing. A good Wife, and a good Husband too, are from the Lord. . . . Please to accept of Mr. Mitchel's Sermons of Glory, which is inclosed." They were married by his son-in-law, and the third Mrs. Sewall outlived him. We hope she cared for him tenderly during these last few years of his life.

Sewall has been called the last of the Puritans; and truly before his death the old order of things had passed away. His last years were a continual protest against the new ideas which were making their way into Boston, of which periwigs were but the outward sign. How it must have wrung his soul to write that the governor gave a ball which lasted till three o'clock in the morning!

What impression do we get of the character of this man who lived two hundred years ago, and whom we know more intimately than any one else that ever walked the streets of Boston? Who of us could stand the test of writing out from day to day, not only our outward actions, but our inward thoughts? What impression would the record make upon posterity two centuries hence? Judge Sewall has stood this test without losing one grain of our respect. The diary is quaint and amusing, sometimes even undignified, and causes many a smile as we linger over its pages; but there is not a single unworthy page in it, not one that we wish had been left unwritten. There are no scandals, no harsh criticisms of contemporaries, no revelations of hypocrisy. One of his last entries is this sentiment from the "New England Weekly Journal": "There is no notion more false than that which some have taken up, that Religion is inconsistent with a Gentleman." May we not leave him with the fitting tribute which Whittier has paid to this magistrate of the olden time, " Samuel Sewall, the good and wise"? —

> "His face with lines of firmness wrought,
> He wears the look of a man unbought,
> Who swears to his hurt and changes not;
> Yet, touched and softened nevertheless
> With the grace of Christian gentleness,
> The face that a child would climb to kiss!
> True and tender and brave and just,
> That man might honor and woman trust.
>
> . . . . . .
>
> Green forever the memory be
> Of the Judge of the old Theocracy,
> Whom even his errors glorified,
> Like a far-seen, sunlit mountain side
> By the cloudy shadows which o'er it glide!
> Honor and praise to the Puritan
> Who the halting step of his age outran.
>
> . . . . . .
>
> To the saintly soul of the early day,
> To the Christian judge, let us turn and say:
> Praise and thanks for an honest man!
> Glory to God for the Puritan!"

SOME DELUSIONS OF OUR FORE-
FATHERS.

SOME DELUSIONS OF OUR FORE-FATHERS.

IF our forefathers had been invariably wise and just and good, they would not have been human. Had they never made mistakes, they would have been too far removed from us. Our own degeneracy would have been too depressing. It is indeed true, as William Stoughton said in his election sermon of 1688, that "God sifted a whole nation, that He might send choice grain into the wilderness." In John Fiske's opinion, there has been, in all history, "no other instance of colonization so exclusively effected by picked and chosen men." In integrity, in earnestness, in that quality which is best expressed by the word, "backbone," they had no peers. Their convictions, their close study of principles, had given them enlarged views on many subjects; but we must not expect them to have been prophets and seers. We must not consider them as a band of chosen philosophers, who had come here to establish advanced ideas. The earnestness which made them willing to endure all manner of persecution, to face banishment and all kind of hardships rather than abandon their convictions, made them, in a sense, narrow. Those convictions were of tremendous importance; they were a matter of life and death; they must be guarded within and without. Hence the expulsion of Ann Hutchinson, of Roger Williams, of the Quakers, and other heretics. It is not in a spirit of criticism that we should examine their mistakes, but in a spirit of inquiry to judge wherein we resemble them. "It is well," says Nevin, "to revive the unwise or unjust acts of our ancestors sometimes, as we would place a beacon on some shoal or reef where a ship had been wrecked, to warn others of the danger."

We have seen that, according to Cotton Mather, the seven enemies with whom New England had to contend were "the Devil, Separatists, Familists, Antinomians, Quakers, clerical impostors, and Indians." All o these were more or less in league with Satan and under his influence. The Indians were his special emissaries, his subjects, and worshippers. When heretics, false prophets, and impostors had been driven out, when the Indians had been repeatedly conquered, and their power lessened, the devil began to tremble lest he was to be driven from his own soil. He roused himself for a mighty effort. The second and third generations of New England had to contend with Satan himself in a terrible conflict for the mastery. For centuries it had been held that the devil was the head and ruler of a world of his own, — a world of demons; that he was able to hold communications with mortals, to interfere in their affairs, and to exercise more or less control over the laws of nature. The logical result of this belief was the belief in demoniacal possession or witchcraft; that is, that a person could sign a compact with Satan, and by this means obtain certain supernatural powers. This belief was by no means confined to the ignorant, the credulous, and the superstitious. It was held by Luther, by Melancthon, and by Kepler. The wisest philosphers, the most eminent scholars, accepted without question the existence of witches. Richard Baxter, whose "Saints' Rest" has soothed so many souls, was a firm believer. Doctor More, Sir Thomas Browne, Boyle, Cranmer, and Bacon were believers. As late as 1765 Blackstone, the great expounder of English law, wrote: "To deny the possibility, nay, actual existence of witchcraft and sorcery, is at once flatly to contradict the revealed word of God in various passages both of the Old and New Testaments; and the thing itself is a truth

DELUSIONS OF OUR FOREFATHERS.

to which every nation in the world hath, in its time, borne testimony either by example, seemingly well attested, or by prohibitory laws which at least suppose the possibility of commerce with evil spirits."

In the seventeenth century a canon in the English Church forbade ministers to cast out devils without a license; and the Bishop of Chester actually issued licenses duly authorizing certain ministers to cast out devils. During this whole century there were trials and executions for witchcraft in all civilized countries. More than two hundred victims were hanged in England; thousands were burned in Scotland, and still larger numbers in France, Germany, and Italy. In Geneva, in 1514, five hundred persons are said to have been executed for witchcraft in two weeks. We have an account of the expenses attending the execution of two witches in Scotland, which shows the cool, matter-of-fact way in which the affair was managed.

For 10 loads of coal to burn them . .	£3	6	8
For a tar barrel	0	14	0
For towes	0	6	0
For hurden to be jumps for them . .	3	11	0
For making of them . . , . . .	0	8	0
For one to go to Fairmouth for the Laird to sit upon their assize as judge .	0	6	0
For the executioner for his pains . .	8	14	0
For his expenses here	0	16	0
Total	18	16	4

Matthew Hopkins in England was so zealous in the matter of exterminating witches that he received the title of "witch finder general." He travelled from place to place; his expenses were paid, and he required in addition regular fees for the discovery of a witch. One of his tests was to prick the body of the accused with pins, to find whether there was a callous spot, which was supposed to be the devil's mark. His favorite test was to tie the thumb of the right hand to the toe of the left foot, and drag the victims through a river or pond; if they floated, they were witches. His success was so great that the people accounted for it by declaring that he had stolen the devil's memorandum book, in which Satan had recorded the names of those who were in league with him. It is some satisfaction to know that his own right thumb and left toe were finally tied together, and he was dragged through a pond. But this did not happen until he had procured the death, in one year, and in one county, of more than three times as many as suffered in Salem during the whole delusion. We see, then, that the witchcraft tragedy in this country was a very small affair compared with those of the Old World, although we have fallen into the habit of speaking of Salem witchcraft as if it were something unique in the history of civilization.

Before we take up this dark history in detail, let us see what witchcraft meant. What constituted a witch? "A witch was a person who had made an actual, deliberate, formal compact with Satan, by which it was agreed that she should become his faithful subject, and do all in her power to aid him in his rebellion against God and his warfare against the gospel and Church of Christ. Thus a witch was considered as a person who had transferred allegiance from God to the devil." Satan was always glad to have these human agents in league with him. In return for their services he bestowed on the witches certain supernatural powers. Through this compact a witch was believed to have the power of afflicting, distressing, and rending whomsoever she would. She could cause them to pine away, throw them into the most frightful convulsions, choke, bruise, pierce, and craze them, subject them to every description of pain and disease, and even to death itself. The persons upon whom she exercised her evil influence were said to be bewitched. The witches could exert this influence at any distance of time or space. When they could not go in person to the ones they wished to afflict, they could transform themselves into the likeness of some animal,—a dog, hog, cat, rat, mouse, or toad, or a yellow bird. They also had imps under their control; and these took the form of an insect, such as a fly or a spider. A witch could also act upon her victims through her spirit, spectre, or apparition. Satan enabled her to be anywhere and everywhere at once. She could also operate on others by means of puppets. She could procure any kind of a doll, and will it to represent the person whom she wished to torment. Then whatever she did to the puppet or doll would be suffered by the person it represented. A pin stuck into the puppet would pierce the flesh of the person she wished to afflict. A witch could also read the thoughts of others, and could influence the minds of those whom she wished to tempt. She could cast the evil eye.

Now let us imagine, for a moment, what the case would be if we believed in the power of human beings to work such evil. What would be our attitude toward them? Are we willing to turn a wild beast loose in our midst? Would we let a small-pox patient roam our streets at will? Would we leave a dangerous lunatic at large? Yet how small the danger from any of these sources compared to what might be expected from the presence of witches. Unless we can place ourselves at this standpoint we cannot realize the terrible panic that swept over New England two hundred years ago. The horror of that tragedy would be unendurable were we not able to remember that the community was mad with terror. Malice and imposture were at work, of course, but the field had been prepared for them. In the case of the Salem tragedies, moreover, it was not simply terror and superstition that actuated our forefathers; it was also the stern determination to meet

Satan face to face and drive him from the land.

There were a number of witches hung in the colonies before the outbreak of the epidemic at Salem. The first execution for witchcraft, in the New World, was in Charlestown, in 1647, the victim being Margaret Jones. Governor Winthrop presided over the trial and pronounced her sentence. He gravely records in his journal the evidence against her, and also the fact that the "same day and hour she was executed, there was a very great tempest at Connecticut which blew down many trees." Mistress Ann Hibbins, of Boston, was sentenced by Governor Endicott. In 1680, Governor Bradstreet sentenced a witch to be hanged, but afterward granted a reprieve, and, though the General Court protested and urged her death, he succeeded in saving the woman's life. Had Governor Bradstreet been in power in 1692, our annals might have been different. He was one of the few enlightened ones who consistently opposed the storm of prejudice. The most interesting witch trial, previous to those at Salem, was that of Goody Glover, an Irish Catholic woman, who was sentenced to death for having bewitched the Goodwin children. These clever little impostors succeeded in fooling the most learned men of Boston, including Cotton Mather, who wrote an account of their strange performances. The writings of the Mathers no doubt helped to arouse a morbid interest in the subject of witchcraft. These earlier cases show that the outbreak at Salem was not phenomenal. It differed in degree, but not in kind, from what was taking place elsewhere. A lack of wisdom in the prominent men led them to foster the excitement rather than check it, and the terrible tragedy followed.

In all the annals of crime there is no more singular story than that of the bewitched children of Salem village. Eight girls, their ages ranging from nine years to eighteen, together with two or three servant girls, procured the death of twenty people and the persecution and imprisonment of at least two hundred more. In our own day we have shuddered at the depravity of a boy criminal like Jesse Pomeroy. Before the depravity of the "bewitched children," as they were called, the mind simply stands appalled, refusing to comprehend. Psychologists can give us no explanation. That these children were deliberate, wicked, cruel impostors there is not a shadow of doubt. It is easy to account for the madness of the community. The history of panics is always the same. But the conduct of the girls who worked up the panic cannot be explained. It would be charitable to suppose them insane, but there is too much proof of method in their madness.

The strange doings began in the house of

the Reverend Mr. Parris, pastor at Salem village. Mr. Parris had formerly lived at the West Indies, and had brought from there three slaves, who were called Indians, but were probably of mixed blood, partly negro. Two of these slaves were concerned in the proceedings. Tituba, the Indian woman, was full of superstitious tales of magic and sorcery belonging to her native tribe. These she poured into the ears of the children of the family, — Elizabeth Parris, aged nine, and her cousin, Abigail Williams, aged eleven. With them was Ann Putnam, aged twelve, the daughter of the clerk of the parish. During the winter of 1691 and '92 these girls, with half a dozen others, some of them servants, met at the house of Mr. Parris and studied palmistry, magic, necromancy, and the like. They absorbed all the lore of Tituba and read all they could find on the subject. They became very proficient in all kinds of juggling tricks. After entertaining themselves for a time, they concluded to astonish their families with their performances. "They would creep into holes and under chairs, writhe in dreadful contortions, utter loud outcries and incoherent unintelligible expressions." Then they added fits, faints, and ravings to their accomplishments. The whole neighborhood was soon filled with the story of their behavior. Their families were alarmed; Dr. Griggs, the village physician, was called in, and, not understanding such unusual symptoms, he gravely declared that the girls were "under an evil eye;" that is, that they were bewitched. Everybody flocked to see the convulsions of the afflicted children. Their love of notoriety increasing, they began to exhibit their fits and ravings in church, which, remarks the Reverend Mr. Lawson with much simplicity, "occurring in public worship did something interrupt me in my first prayer, being so unusual." On a certain Sunday Abigail Williams cried out after the psalm, "Now stand up and take your text!" then, "It's a long text!" Another, in the middle of the discourse, exclaimed, "Now there is enough of that!" One called out, " Look where she sits upon the beam, sucking her yellow bird betwixt her fingers;" and another, " There is a yellow bird sitting on the minister's hat as it hangs in the pulpit."

Instead of being punished for such performances, the girls were looked upon with pity and terror. Mr. Parris was greatly exercised. He invited the neighboring ministers to his house for a day of fasting and prayer. The children performed before them. The ministers were amazed and horror stricken. They confirmed the decision of the doctor that the children were under the power of the devil; that is, they were bewitched. The community was wildly excited. They felt that the evil one was let loose among them. As he could operate only through human beings in league with him, it was necessary to know who his agents were. "Who is the devil's agent bewitching these unfortunate girls?" was the cry. They were importuned to tell who had hurt them. At first they were loth to accuse any one, but being pressed, named Good, Osborne, and Tituba. Their victims were cleverly chosen. Three more friendless people could not be found. Sarah Good was a bedridden beggar, who had separated from her husband and was universally disliked. Sarah Osborne was another helpless old woman, who had made an unhappy marriage, was shattered in mind, and had been the subject of much scandal. Tituba, the Indian woman, was an excellent tool. Warrants were issued for the arrest of the three women, and they were brought before the magistrates to be examined.

The examination was to be held in the tavern, but such crowds came out that they had to adjourn to the meeting-house. The multitude were filled with excitement and abhorrence. The magistrates, John Hathorne and Jonathan Corwin, seated themselves in front of the pulpit, facing the audience. Before them was a table or raised platform, and on this the first prisoner, Sarah Good, was placed, to be out of reach of the crowd and in plain sight. The magistrates assumed from the first that the prisoners were guilty, and framed their questions in that view, trying to make them confess or contradict themselves. The afflicted children were brought in as witnesses and placed before the prisoner. When the poor old woman, from her table, looked down upon them, they fell to the floor as if struck dead, or screeched in agony; or went into fearful spasms and convulsive fits; or cried out that they were pricked with pins, pinched, and throttled by invisible hands. Each one was brought up to the prisoner, touched her person, and was at once restored to calm and quiet. With one voice they all declared that Sarah Good had thus tormented them by her power as a witch in league with the devil. We may imagine the excitement of the crowd as they saw the effect produced before their eyes, and saw how, upon touching her, the diabolical effects ceased, the malignant fluid passing back like an electric stream into the body of the witch. No other evidence was needed to prove her guilt. She was carried to prison, bound with cords, and loaded with irons; for it was thought that fastenings would not hold a witch. The proceedings in the case of Sarah Osborne were exactly the same. The children were brought in, repeated the acting, and fixed the delusion more firmly in the minds of the crowd.

When Tituba was brought upon the stand, the wily Indian confessed, and accused the other two of being her accomplices and of having forced her to sign the devil's book. She repeated to those grave magistrates and to the awe-struck multitude strange tales of riding through the air on sticks, with Good and Osborne behind her; of having imps who did their bidding; of familiar spirits in the shape of cats, dogs, and yellow birds, which they sent to hurt and afflict the bewitched girls. Day by day the same scenes were repeated. The magistrates, with their cavalcade, came in pomp from Salem to Salem village, every morning, and the prisoners were brought on horseback from the Ipswich jail, — a distance of ten miles, — and carried back at night. The examination each day was simply a repetition, with the actions of the girls as proof positive of the guilt of the accused. While Tituba was confessing, their torments ceased. When she had finished she herself fell into convulsions, declaring that the devil was punishing her for her confessions.

Tituba had said that there were four women and two men in the league, and it was necessary to find the other two. The girls, having gained such an influence, became bolder in their charges and aimed higher. Their next victim was Martha Corey, an honored member of the church, against whom there was not a shadow of blame. She had incurred their ill-will by declaring her unbelief in witchcraft. They feared the clear eyes which could see their imposture, and decided to put her out of the way by calling her a witch. The fourth was Frances Nourse, a mother in Israel, and a disbeliever in witchcraft.

At this stage, Deodat Lawson, a former pastor, arrived in the village and preached a memorable sermon on the all-engrossing theme. With impassioned eloquence he summoned the people of God to rally and confront unflinchingly their hellish foe. The effect of his sermon was terrible. Awe, anger, consternation, and frantic zeal filled the hearts of his hearers. The Reverend Mr. Parris also preached on the subject, from the text, "Have I not chosen you twelve and one of you is a devil?" It was communion Sunday. Sarah Cloyse, the sister of Frances Nourse, was present. The sister who had sat with her on the last communion day was now chained in prison, "awaiting the horrors of a frenzied tribunal." She felt that the text was a fling at her sister, and her heart was too full to remain. She arose and passed out of the meeting-house to her home. From that day she, too, was marked as a witch, and her doom was sealed. Other charges followed. A child four years old was placed in prison. No one was safe, high or low. The Reverend Mr. Burroughs, a former pastor, was declared a witch, and brought from Maine for his trial. A council from the General Court, consisting of the deputy governor and five magistrates, came out to inquire into the matter. The prisons were almost full of those who had signed the devil's book. Panic prevailed everywhere. People began to feel that their only safety lay in accusing others. Many confessed to save themselves. Business was at a standstill. Many quit the country.

Just at this crisis, Sir William Phipps arrived in Boston, the new Governor chosen by Increase Mather. The new charter, which made Massachusetts a royal province instead of an independent colony, was put in force. A more unsuitable man for such an emergency could not have been found. Ignorant, credulous, and superstitious, he increased the frenzy instead of assuaging it. His first order was that heavy irons should be put upon all those in prison. Salem jails were now full of those awaiting final trial. The governor appointed a special court of Oyer and Terminer to try them, consisting of seven judges, with Lieutenant-Governor Stoughton as Chief Justice.

Many were the tests by which a witch was discovered. It was believed that a witch could not weep, could not shed tears. If then the accused were too dazed or angry to weep, it told against them. Again, it was believed that when they signed the infernal compact, the devil put his mark upon them by touching with his finger some part of the body. His touch left a callous spot which could not feel pain. A committee was appointed of each sex to examine the bodies of the accused. The only way of testing them was by sticking pins into them to find the callous spot or the devil's mark. There was also the test by water, already spoken of. "If you float, you are a witch: if you sink, you are not." This was not much used in Salem. But the worst thing was the spectral evidence. It was believed that a witch could be present in her spectre or apparition at any place she pleased, no matter what the distance. If, then, the afflicted testified that they had been tormented by the shape of any person, it was of no use to prove an alibi, for a witch could easily be in two or three places at once.

If she did not wish to go herself, she could send her imp, in the shape of a dog, cat, toad, rat, spider, or bird; or she could roll up a bundle of rags into a puppet, and by sticking pins into it could torment whomsoever she would.

Then there was the visible evidence of the effect of the presence of the accused upon the afflicted. As soon as a prisoner was brought in, the girls fell into convulsions and ravings. If, in her terror, she clasped her hands, they would shriek out that she was pinching them. When she pressed her lips, they exclaimed that she was biting them. If in her weariness she leaned to one side or the other, they cried out that their bodies were crushed. If she took a step or changed her position, they would say their feet were in pain. When Goody Nourse's head drooped to one side from fatigue, their necks were bent the same way. Elizabeth Hubbard's neck was fixed in that direction and could not be moved. Abigail Williams cried out, "Set up Goody Nourse's head, the maid's neck will be broke." Whereupon some one held the prisoner's head up and Betty Hubbard's was immediately righted. The afflicted girls also declared that they were pricked with pins, and the pins drawn from under their flesh were produced in court. These pins are still preserved in Salem in the court-house. They are kept in a glass bottle, sealed with the court seal. Sometimes the evidence was so appalling that the amazed prisoners were led to believe in their own guilt.

Against such testimony as this no plea that they could make would be of any avail. To be accused meant to be convicted. The verdict was a foregone conclusion. In the case of Frances Nourse, the jury were so impressed by the age, character, and bearing of the woman that they brought in a verdict of not guilty. Immediately there was an outcry from the accusers and the spectators. Whereupon the magistrates sent the jury back to find another verdict, and they were obliged to pronounce her guilty. After her condemnation the governor granted her a reprieve; but the people of Salem prevailed upon him to recall it, and she was executed with the rest. After the sentence was passed, she was, by a unanimous vote of the parish, formally excommunicated from the church, of which she had been for more than fifty years an honored member. There is a tradition that her body, instead of being thrown into the pit on Gallows Hill, was stolen away by her children and buried at the home. A beautiful monument now marks her grave, and two years ago her descendants, to the number of hundreds, celebrated the two hundredth anniversary of her martyrdom.

Among the saddest cases of this series of tragedies are those of Martha Corey and her husband, Giles Corey. Mrs. Corey was an earnest, sincere Christian, and too enlightened for the age in which she lived. She was one of the two or three bold ones who dared to say that they did not believe in witches. This disbelief was enough in itself to cast suspicion on her. A person who did not believe in witchcraft was considered almost an infidel. A member of the Royal Society in England but a few years before had written, "Atheism is begun in Sadducism. And those that dare not bluntly say 'there is no God,' content themselves, for a fair step and introduction, to deny there are spirits or witches!" Giles Corey, the husband, had been a hard, rough man all his life, and had engaged in quarrels and lawsuits; but, a year or two before, when over eighty years of age, he had joined the church. He was completely carried away by the excitement. He left his work, day after day, to attend the first examinations. When his wife spoke freely and fearlessly against the delusions, and begged him to stay away from the trials, he was horrified at her infidelity. When the wretched children cried out upon her as a witch, the superstitious old man began to fear there was some truth in it. He remembered that she often remained kneeling on the hearthstone a long time after he had gone to bed. He remembered accidents that had happened to his ox and his cat. He remembered that his saddle had sometimes disappeared when he wanted to go to the trials. He remembered that recently, when he tried to pray, he could not think of anything to say, and he feared he was bewitched; not realizing, poor old man, that when one has been for eighty years unaccustomed to prayer, the habit may not come easily. All these unguarded expresssions of his were used against Mrs. Corey. The greatest excitement prevailed at her trial. One hysterical woman threw her muff at her, and, missing her aim, took off her shoe and threw it, hitting Mrs.

Corey on the head. Two of Corey's sons-in-law testified against her. Martha Corey was committed to prison; was tried, and sentenced to death. "Protesting her inocency, she concluded her life with prayer upon the ladder."

Giles Corey had scarcely awakened from his delusion and realized the terrible fate that awaited his wife, when he himself was marked as a victim. He had probably spoken too freely of her condemnation. Knowing that there was no hope of justice, and that to be accused meant certain death, he resolved upon a heroic course. He had four married daughters. Two of his sons-in-law had testified against his wife. He wished to show his attitude to those who had been false to her and to those who had been true. He therefore made a will, in prison, which was rather a deed, conveying all his property to the two who had upheld his wife in her trouble. He feared, however, that if he were tried and convicted of felony the will would not stand, and his property would be confiscated. He determined not to be brought to trial. He chose a course which required all the courage and firmness of which a human being is capable. When called into court to answer to the indictment found by the grand jury, he would neither plead guilty nor not guilty, but stood mute. Unless he would plead, there could be no trial; and he would thus retain the power of disposing of his own property, and securing it to his daughters. To deprive the public of the excitement of the trial, to deprive the magistrates of their right of convicting him, to deprive the afflicted children of the privilege of being afflicted in his presence, was the most exasperating plan he could have taken. But in spite of the wrath and amazement of the magistrates and people, nothing could unseal his lips. For such an offence, which was called "standing dumb," the English law provided a penalty. "In such cases the prisoner was to be three times brought before the court, and called to plead; the consequences of persisting in standing mute being solemnly announced to him each time. If he remained obdurate the sentence of *peine forte et dure* was passed upon him; and, remanded to prison, he was placed in a low and dark apartment. He would there be laid on his back on the bare floor, naked for the most part. A weight of iron would be placed upon him, not quite enough to crush him. He would have no sustenance, save only, on the first day, three morsels of the worst bread; and on the second day, three draughts of standing water that should be nearest to the prison door; and, in this situation, such would be alternately his daily diet till he died, or till he answered." The object of this punishment was to induce the prisoner to plead to the indictment, so that he could be brought to trial in the ordinary way. The practice of putting weights upon the victims, and gradually increasing the weight, was to force them, by the slowly increasing torture, to yield. Giles Corey, a man over eighty years of age, voluntarily faced this horrible lingering death, rather than yield his rights or recognize the justice of that frenzied tribunal. His heroism made a profound impression on the minds of the public, and had its influence in breaking the spell which bound them.

During all these proceedings the afflicted girls had grown more and more expert in their acting. Their continual public exhibitions had increased their boldness and their skill. No necromancer could surpass them in the management of voice and feature, in sleight of hand, in the simulation of passions, sufferings, and physical affections. "There has seldom been better acting in a theatre than they displayed in the presence of the astonished and horror-stricken rulers, magistrates, ministers, judges, jurors, spectators, and prisoners. Day by day pastors, deacons, church members, college professors, officers of state, everybody, learned and ignorant, crowded into the church to behold their feats; feats which have scarcely ever been surpassed either by ancient sorcerers and magicians, or by modern jugglers and mesmerizers." No one seems to have dreamed that their actings and sufferings could be the result of cunning or imposture. The accused themselves were utterly confounded by the acting of the girls, and almost began to feel that they had been the instruments of the evil one without knowing it. "To see a young woman or girl suddenly struck down, speechless, pallid as in death; with muscles rigid, eyeballs fixed or rolled back in their sockets; the stiffened frame either wholly prostrated or drawn up into contorted attitudes and shapes, or vehemently convulsed with racking pains, or dropping with relaxed muscles into a lifeless lump; and to hear dread shrieks of delirious ravings, must have produced a truly frightful effect upon an excited and deluded assembly. The constables and their assistants would go to the rescue, lift the body of the sufferer, and bear it in their arms toward the prisoner. The magistrates and the crowd, hushed in the deepest silence, would watch with breathless awe the result of the experiment. The officers slowly approached the accused, who, when they came near, would, in obedience to the order of the magistrates, hold out a hand and touch the flesh of the afflicted one. Instantly the spasms cease, the eyes open, color returns to the countenance, the limbs resume their position and functions, and life and intelligence are wholly restored. The sufferer comes to herself, walks back, and takes her seat as well as ever." No wonder the effect on the accused persons was confounding, and that it sometimes broke them down. Poor Deliverance Hobbs was completely overpowered. Both reason and conscience seemed to abandon her. Exclaiming, "I am amazed, I am amazed!" she assented to every charge brought against her, and said whatever she was told to say.

The afflicted children had become the autocrats of the village. There was no limit to their boldness. They were no longer cautious as to where they should strike. No aim was too high for them. Dudley Bradstreet, son of the honored and revered Simon Bradstreet who had so long served as governor, was obliged to flee. Suspicion was cast upon Lady Phipps, wife of Sir William Phipps, the governor, who had openly sympathized with the prisoners. Capt. John Alden, son of John Alden of the "Mayflower," was brought from Boston to Salem to stand a trial. There is a satisfaction in reading the somewhat strong and emphatic sailor language which Captain Alden addressed to the magistrates on this occasion. He was placed in prison, but made his escape, and fled to his relatives in Duxbury, where he remained in hiding until the storm had passed by. The old sailor could never afterward speak of the episode with any degree of calmness.

The reign of terror had lasted for more than six months; twenty people had been put to death, — nineteen by hanging, and one by being pressed to death; two had died in prison, from fright and exhaustion. When eight had been hanged in one day on Gallows Hill, the Rev. Mr. Noyes, pointing to their bodies, exclaimed: "What a sad sight to see eight firebrands of hell hanging there!" The prisons of Boston, Salem, Cambridge, and Ipswich were full, and had been for months. Hundreds had been committed, and were awaiting their trial. One victim had been executed in June, five in July, five in August, and eight in September.

Suddenly the storm seemed to have spent itself. The people awakened from the horrible nightmare which had weighed upon them. There is no other instance in history of so sudden, so rapid, so complete a revulsion of feeling. The first examination on the charge of witchcraft was held on the first day of March. The last execution occurred on the twenty-second of September. In September the special court adjourned, to meet again in a few weeks; but it never met again. Governor Phipps, seeing the temper of the people, abolished the special court. In the following January, at the session of the Superior Court of Judicature in Salem, the grand jury brought in fifty indictments for witchcraft; but only three were convicted, and these were never executed. Later, four were tried in Charlestown, one in Boston, and five in Ipswich; but no convictions could be secured. It was not the officials who had changed, but the people. The jurors repeatedly refused to convict. When Judge Stoughton, who had presided over both courts, found that he was not to be allowed to sentence any more witches, he was so exasperated that he left the bench in displeasure and never returned. "Word was brought that a reprieve was sent to Salem, and had prevented the execution of seven of those that were condemned, which so moved the chief judge that he said to this effect: 'We were in a way to have cleared the land of them; who it is that obstructs the cause of justice I know not; the Lord be merciful to the country!' and so went off the bench, and came no more into that court."

One thing that helped to turn the tide of public opinion was the accusation brought against Mrs. Hale, wife of the Rev. Mr. Hale, of Beverly. Mr. Hale had helped to raise the storm, had been zealous in urging it on; but when it broke over his own household, he turned and resisted it. Mrs. Hale was so universally beloved and esteemed, her character was so far above reproach, that even that frenzied community refused to believe her guilty. They began to feel that the accusers had perjured themselves, and from that moment their power was at an end. At Andover, where more than fifty were in prison, the accused, taking advantage of the turn of the tide, began to bring suits for slander against the accusers. There were some zealots, of course, who tried to keep up the excitement, but they did not succeed. The storm had spent itself. The reaction had set in. It was not that people had ceased to believe in the reality of witchcraft. Even Calef, the most bitter contemporary critic of the trials, wrote, a year later: "That there are witches is not the doubt. The scriptures else were vain . . . but what this witchcraft is and wherein it does consist, seems to be the whole difficulty." The great change seemed to be the distrust of spectral evidence. When any one had testified that the apparition of such and such a person had appeared to him and had afflicted and tormented him, and that he had known this apparition to commit murders and all sorts of crimes, it was received as evidence. It was held that the devil could not assume the shape of any person unless that person were willing and in league with him. It was of no use then for the accused to prove that, at the time in question, he was in an entirely different place; for the crime could be committed by his apparition as well as by himself. They now began to say that the devil could assume any shape he chose, even that of a perfectly good and innocent man. As soon as spectral evidence was thrown out, the witch trials fell through.

In May, 1693, Governor Phipps issued a proclamation ordering the release from prison of all who were held on the charge of witchcraft. "Such a jail delivery was never known in New England." One hundred and fifty came out of the prisons. To the disgrace of the courts, only those were released who had paid their board during the entire time of their imprisonment, and their jailer's fees. Those who had not the means were left to languish in jail until some one paid these dues for them. Tituba, the Indian woman, was finally sold for her fees.

We cannot ascertain definitely how many had suffered from the charge; for, besides those who had been put to death, those who had been released, and those who had been left for their fees, there were many who were out on bail, and others who had escaped from prison. Some, too, had fled from the country, when suspicion was cast upon them, without allowing themselves to be examined. Probably no less than three hundred people had been definitely charged with witchcraft by that one circle of girls.

Those who were released had been for

many months in a prison cell, heavily chained. Their property had been wasted, their families scattered, their health broken. Their freedom was restored; but what was to compensate for their ruined lives? A few years later the General Court reversed the attainder against those who had been executed, and tried to make good to their families the losses suffered. The churches also revoked the sentences of excommunication. In 1697 the government appointed a public fast-day throughout the colony, to implore the Lord to turn away his anger, and not to punish the land for that fatal error. The jurors who had tried and convicted the accused made a public statement, confessing that they had been "sadly deluded and mistaken."

As to the girls who had originated the horrible tragedy, most of them turned out profligates. Only one of them — Ann Putnam — ever made public confession of her sin; and this confession was not so humble as it might have been, considering the ruin she had wrought.

The Rev. Mr. Parris persisted in the delusion with which his name will forever be associated. The people of Salem village made heroic efforts to rid themselves of his ministry, but he refused to go. All the ministers of Boston had to be called in before the community could be rid of his presence. As we think of those who were condemned, one thing must be remembered to their everlasting honor, — namely, that confession at any time would have saved them. They preferred to die rather than to lie. Some, who at first were, through weakness, persuaded or terrified into a confession, afterward voluntarily took it back and disowned it before trial. "It required great strength of mind to take back a confession; relinquish life and liberty; go down into a dungeon loaded with irons; and thence to ascend the gallows." Yet many a weak girl took this step rather than live with that terrible lie on her soul.

And the people who were carried away with this weird tide of fanaticism, — can we realize how the loneliness of their surroundings, the isolation of their lives, the dangers with which they were beset, and the hardships they had to endure, formed their minds, and made them a suitable prey for gloomy fancies and morbid superstitions? In the history of this panic is there any resemblance to the action of mobs in our own day? It is easy to stand upon a pinnacle of superiority and look down with a pitying smile upon the delusions of our forefathers; but, after all, are we free enough from superstition, passion, and prejudice to pass judgment upon them?

A GROUP OF PURITAN POETS.

A GROUP OF PURITAN POETS.

TO most of us the words Puritan and poet seem antagonistic, — the one a contradiction of the other. The traditional Puritan is a long-faced, sour-visaged man, clad in sad-colored garments. He sternly represses in himself, and in those about him, all expression of natural affection, all longing for the beautiful, all desire for enjoyment and pleasure. Macaulay tells us that the Puritan hated bear-baiting, not because it gave pain to the bears, but because it gave pleasure to the spectators. One hundred and fifty years ago the poet, Freneau, expressed the popular idea of the Puritan: —

"There exiles were formed in a whimsical mould
And were awed by their priests like the Hebrews of old,
Disclaimed all pretenses to jesting and laughter,
And sighed their lives through to be happy hereafter.

On a crown immaterial their thoughts were intent,
They looked toward Zion where-ever they went,
Did all things in hope of a future reward,
And worried mankind — for the sake of the Lord."

Hawthorne describes the Puritan children playing on the doorstep in such grim fashion as their training would permit, — playing at going to church, or at scourging Quakers, or at fighting Indians, or at taking witches. In short, all our ideas of the Puritan combine to suggest a life of repression and gloom. We sometimes fear that we have inherited from them a sort of vague and undefined belief that " if you are good you will be happy, but you won't have a good time."

Was there any place for poetry on this sombre background? What is poetry without the idea of the beautiful, without the natural emotions of the heart? Had the Puritan then no heart? Had he no warm human blood? If you want to know the real Puritan without his shell, turn away from those musty volumes of sermons, which it would require "a long life, implicit faith, and more than the patience of Job" to read through, and study rather the quaint old diaries and the letters of these men who crossed the ocean, for the sake of their convictions. Read, for instance, this farewell letter, written by Governor Winthrop to the wife whom he was leaving behind in England until he could prepare a home for her in the wilderness: —

"And now (my sweet soul) I must once again take my last fare-well of thee in Old England. It goeth very near to my heart to leave thee; but I know to whom I have committed thee, even to Him who loves thee much better than any husband can, who hath taken account of the hairs of thy head, and puts all thy tears in his bottle, who can and (if it be for his glory) will, bring us together again with peace and comfort. Oh, how it refresheth my heart, to think that I shall yet again see thy sweet face in the land of the living! — that lovely countenance, that I have so much delighted in, and beheld with so great content! I have hitherto been so taken up with business, as I could seldom look back to my former happiness; but now, when I shall be at some leisure, I shall not avoid the remembrance of thee, nor the grief for thy absence. Thou hast thy share with me, but I hope the course we have agreed upon will be some ease to us both. Mondays and Fridays, at five of the clock at night, we shall meet in spirit till we meet in person. Yet, if all these hopes should fail, blessed be our God, that we are assured we shall meet one day, if not as husband and wife, yet in a better condition. Let that stay and comfort thy heart. Neither can the sea drown thy husband, nor enemies destroy, nor any adversity deprive thee of thy husband or children. Therefore I will only take thee now and my sweet children in mine arms, and kiss and embrace you all, and so leave you with my God. Fare-well, fare-well. I bless you all in the name of the Lord Jesus."

Can any woman of the present day show a more tender love-letter? More demonstrative ones we may find, perhaps, more full of extravagant expressions, but none that show a warmer, truer heart. Indeed, the more closely we study the Puritan, the more human we find him. There is plenty of evidence that he had a heart, though it may have been sometimes overshadowed by his conscience. The greatest fault of the Puritan seems to have been an excess of earnestness. He was so terribly in earnest in his beliefs and purposes that he had no time to make life pleasant and easy for himself or his family. Lowell has summed up the Puritan's creed in three points, — "faith in God, faith in man, and faith in work." He might also have added, faith in the devil; for it was his firm belief in the ever-present activity and enmity of the devil that accounted for his austerity. It was not from hardness of heart that he tried to repress all worldly instincts in his children, but from a watchful and jealous love which would save them, in spite of themselves, from the grasp of Satan.

The Puritan prejudice against art and against beauty was also a matter of conscience. It was the natural reaction against the beauty worship of the Renaissance. On the one hand were the immorality and the paganizing tendencies of the Renaissance, on the other, the Catholic reverence for paintings and shrines and grand cathedrals. In his intense desire to escape these two dangers, the Puritan had really come to believe that the Lord loved angles better than curves, and that ugliness was more pleasing in his sight than beauty. Painting and sculpture and architecture, then, were not for him. There remained only poetry and music, and these with certain limitations. Dramatic poetry, the writings of Shakespeare and his brother playwrights and actors, must be passed by as temptations of the evil one. There was left only the metaphysical school, with its curious quirks and conceits and plays upon words. As to music,— the instrumental music used in church worship in the old country "savored of popery." It was a part of the "bare and beggarly ceremonies" which they had sought to escape. We may judge what they thought of choirs from Puritan Prynnes' description of them: "Choirsters bellow the tenor as it were oxen; bark a counterpart as it were a kennel of dogs; roar out a treble as it were a sort of bulls; and grunt a bass, as it were a number of hogs."

It will be seen that the field allowed to the Puritan poet was a very narrow one indeed. Yet the desire for poetic expression must be a natural instinct of the human heart; for, in spite of all these restrictions and prejudices, the Puritans wrote verses by the hundred, — not a poem now and then, but quires of them, reams of them, miles of them. Not an isolated genius here and there, breaking out irrepressibly into song, but every one — preachers, governors, artisans — found vent in rhyme. It was said of John Wilson, the first pastor of Boston, that he had so nimble a faculty of putting his devout thoughts into verse, that he signalized himself by sending poems to all persons, in all places, on all occasions, wherein the curious relished the piety, sometimes, rather than the poetry. His epitaph commends to after ages, —

"His care to guide his flock and feed his lambs,
By words, works, prayers, psalms, alms, and anagrams."

The first considerable collection of poetry of the forefathers was that poetic prodigy, that metrical monstrosity known as the "Bay Psalm Book," which enjoys the distinction of being the first book published in New England. The Pilgrims had brought from Holland a few copies of Ainsworth's version of the Psalms; but it was not adopted by other churches because the tunes were too difficult, and because it did not contain all the psalms. The Puritans had brought some copies of Sternhold and Hopkin's version; but this was objectionable for the reason that it was used in the Church of England, and also because it was not literal enough. They decided to have a version of their own for use in the churches, and appointed a committee

A GROUP OF PURITAN POETS. 243

to prepare it, consisting of the "chiefest divines of the country." It seems appropriate that the first book printed in Massachusetts should be a psalm book. It was printed in Cambridge in 1640, and was used by the New England churches for more than a century. The titlepage is as follows: —

"The Whole Book of Psalmes Faithfully Translated into English Metre. Whereunto is prefixed a discourse declaring not only the lawfulness, but also the necessity of the Heavenly Ordinance of Singing Psalmes in the Churches of God.

Coll. III. Let the word of God dwell plenteously in you in all wisdome, teaching and exhorting one another in Psalmes, Himnes, and spirituall Songs, singing to the Lord with grace in your hearts.

James V. If any be afflicted, let him pray; and if any be merry let him sing psalmes."

The words, "for the Use Edification and Comfort of the saints, in Public and Private, especially in New England," were added to the second edition. The book was sung through in course, beginning with the first psalm; and when the end was reached, they went back to the first again. There was no thought of adapting the psalm to the sermon. Eight tunes were used for the whole book, — namely, Oxford, Litchfield, Low Dutch, York, Windsor, Cambridge, Saint David's, and Martyrs. Since there were only a few in each congregation who were able to own the book, the deacon "lined the psalm." This sometimes made queer breaks in the meaning of the words. For instance, the deacon would read: "The Lord will come and he will not," and the people would sing, and then pause for the second line,—"keep silence but speak out." There was much discussion at first as to whether the men only should sing, and not the women. "Because it is not permitted to a woman to speak in the church, how then shall they sing? Much less is it permitted them to prophecy in the church and singing of psalms is a kind of prophecying." The Rev. John Cotton answered these objections, and the women sang. Some of the psalms were one hundred and thirty lines long; and the lining and the singing occupied a full half hour, the congregation standing meanwhile. Yet Judge Sewall, in his diary, frequently makes "Humbell acknowledgement to God of the great comfort and merciful kindness received through singing his psalms."

Having seen how the Puritans sang, let us look at what they sang, — the metrical and poetical translations produced by their "chief divines." Here is a part of the fifty-eighth psalm: —

> "The wicked are estranged from
> the womb, they goe astray
> as soon as ever they are borne;
> uttering lyes are they.

> "Their poyson's like serpent's poyson.
> They like deafe Aspe, her eare
> that stops. Thuough charmer wisely charme
> his voice she will not heare.

> "Within their mouth doe thou their teeth
> break out, O God most strong,
> doe thou Jehovah, the great teeth
> break of the lion's young."

A verse of the fifty-first psalm will illustrate the good men's struggles for rhyme: —

> " Create in me clean heart at last God:
> A right spirit in me new make.
> Nor from thy presence quite me cast,
> thy holy spright not from me take."

But, for both metre and rhyme, their crowning effort was the rendering of the one hundred and thirty-third psalm: —

> "1. How good and sweet to see
> i'ts for bretheren to dwell
> together in unitee:
>
> "2. Its like choice oyle that fell
> the head upon
> that down did flow
> the beard unto
> beard of Aron:
> The skirts of his garment
> that unto him went down:
>
> "3. Like Hermons dews descent
> Sions mountains upon
> for there to bee
> the Lords blessing
> Life aye lasting
> commandeth hee."

From the rhythm of this we can understand some of Judge Sewall's difficulties in setting the tune. "He spake to me to set the tune," he records. "I intended Windsor and fell into High Dutch, and then essaying another tune went into a key much too high. So I prayed Mr. White to set the tune which he did well. Litchfield." Again he writes: "I set York tune and the congregation went out of it into St. David's in the very 2d going over." Another time he set Windsor tune, and they "ran over into Oxford do what I would."

Bound up in the back of the third edition of the psalm-book were some scripture songs from other parts of the Bible. Here is a portion of the song of Deborah and Barak: —

"24 Jael the Kenite Hebers wife
'bove women blest shall be:
Above the women in the tent
a blessed one is she.
25 He water ask'd: she gave him milk
him butter forth she fetch'd
26 In Lordly dish: then to the nail
she forth her left hand stretched.

> "Hĕr right the workman's hammer held
>   and Sisera struck dead:
> She pierced and struck his temple through
>   and then smote off his head.
> 27 He at her feet bow'd, fell, lay down
>   he at her feet bow'd, where
> He fell: Ev'n where he bowed down
>   he fell destroyed there."

Whenever Judge Sewall attended a wedding, he was accustomed to carry as a bridal gift a copy of this psalm-book, and to sing from it, to the gloomy tune of Windsor, the hymn known as "Myrrh Aloes":—

> "8 Myrrh Aloes and Cassias smell
>   all of thy garments had
> out of the yvory pallaces
>   whereby they made thee glad:
>
> "9 Amongst thine honorable maids
>   kings daughters present were
> The Queen is set at thy right hand
>   in fine gold of Ophir."

He then presented the book to the bridegroom with words like these:—

"I give you this Psalm Book in order to your perpetuating this Song; and I would have you pray that it may be an introduction to our Singing with the Choir above."

The Puritans had been singing the psalms to their eight tunes for about ten years, when the poems of Anne Bradstreet appeared. What wonder that the unhappy New Englanders hailed her with delight as the "Tenth Muse;" for it must be remembered that the first professional poet of New England was a woman. She was, too, a Puritan of the Puritans. The daughter of that austere old Puritan, Gov. Thomas Dudley, and the wife of the equally strict, but less stern Puritan, Simon Bradstreet, she had known from her childhood no other influence. In 1630 she came, a young bride in her "teens," to America; and most of her poems were written during the first ten years in the wilderness. But they do not tell us what we should so much like to know, — her impressions of this strange New World, her hardships, trials, and adventures in it. Her pen does not deal with any such common, everyday subjects, but seeks far more ambitious themes, as may be seen from the following elaborate titlepage prefixed by her friends to the first edition of her poems: —

"THE TENTH MUSE — Lately sprung up in America. or Severall Poems, compiled with great variety of Wit and Learning, full of delight. Wherein especially is contained a complete discourse and description of

The Four { Elements, Constitutions, Ages of Man, Seasons of the year.

Together with an Exact Epitomie of the Four Monarchies, viz.

The { Assyrian, Persian, Grecian, Roman.

Also a Dialogue between Old England and New, concerning the late troubles. With divers other pleasant and serious Poems. By a Gentlewoman in those parts. Printed at London for Stephen Bowtell at the signe of the Bible in Popes Head-Alley. 1650."

A preface, written by a masculine hand, commends the book and prophesies that men will envy the excellency of the inferior sex, and will even question whether it be a woman's work, and ask, —

"Is it possible? If any do, take this as an answer from him that dares avow it; it is the Work of a Woman, honoured and esteemed where she lives, for her gracious demeanour, her eminent parts, her pious conversation, her courteous disposition, her exact diligence in her place, and discreet managing of her Family occasions, and more then so, these Poems are the fruit but of some few houres, curtailed from her sleep and other refreshments."

Following the preface were a number of poetic eulogies from prominent clergymen who had read the poems in manuscript. John Rogers informs her that twice he has drunk the nectar of her lines, and speaks of "weltring in delight." Another writes: —

"I've read your Poem (Lady) and admire,
Your Sex to such a pitch should e'er aspire;
Go on to write, continue to relate,
New Historyes, of Monarchy and State.

> And what the Romans to their Poets gave
> Be sure such honour and esteem you'l have."

And another still: —

> "Twere extream folly should I dare attempt,
> To praise this Author's worth with complement;
> None but her self must dare commend her parts,
> Whose sublime brain's the Synopsis of Arts.
> Nature and skill, here both in one agree,
> To frame this Master-piece of Poetry:
> False Fame, belye their Sex no more, it can
> Surpass, or parallel the best of Man."

The Rev. Nathaniel Ward, of Ipswich, who had small esteem for women, wrote: —

> "It half revives my chil frost-bitten blood,
> To see a Woman once, do aught that's good;
> And chode by Chaucers Boots, and Homers Furrs
> Let Men look to 't, least Women wear the Spurrs."

Anne herself, in her prologue, forestalls those who might object to a woman's wielding a pen: —

> "I am obnoxious to each carping tongue
> Who says my hand a needle better fits,
> A Poets pen all scorn I thus should wrong,
> For such despite they cast on Female wits:
> If what I do prove well, it won't advance,
> They'l say it's stoln, or else it was by chance."

We are now ready for the poems themselves. They are divided, as we have seen from the titlepage, into quaternions. The first group considers the four elements — Fire, Earth, Air, and Water — represented as four personages who have met together, and are quarrelling for the precedence, each glorifying his own deeds and belittling the others. Fire stands forth and recounts her services to mankind, — how she has framed his tools, forged his weapons, cast his pots and kettles, cooked his food and warmed his limbs. She then describes her powers, — how she has destroyed cities and turned castles to cinders, — speaks of the terrors of her volcanoes, and concludes: —

"What shall I say of Lightning and of Thunder
Which Kings and mighty ones amaze with wonder,
Which make a Cæsar (Romes) the worlds proud
    head,
Foolish Caligula creep under's bed.
And in a word, the world I shall consume
And all therein at that great day of Doom."

Fire sits down satisfied, and Earth arises to make her plea. She describes at great length her mountains, hills, and dales, her fruits and flowers, the many commodities she produces for man, and, like Fire, concludes her bragging with a threat: —

> "I 'le say no more, but this thing add I must
> Remember Sons, your mould is of my dust
> And after death whether interr'd or burn'd
> As Earth at first so into Earth return'd."

Water angrily takes her place. She mentions proudly her fountains, rivers, lakes, and ponds, her sundry seas, — black and white, — her curative springs, her tides, her dews, concluding with a reference to the flood, when "wholly perish'd Earths ignoble race." Then Air, calm and placid, takes her stand: —

> "I do suppose you 'l yield without controul,
> I am the breath of every living soul."

Air goes on to show that words are but wind; the sound of drums, trumpets, and organs are but forced air; also the report of the gun and your songs and pleasant tunes,—they are the same. Air fills the bellows of the smith and the sails of the mariner, and so on.

After the four elements come the four ages of man.

> "What gripes of wind mine infancy did pain,
> What tortures I in breeding teeth sustain?"

sings the first age of man; and the afflicted third age cries:—

> "The Cramp and Gout doth sadly torture me,
> And the restraining lame Sciatica.
> The Astma, Megrim, Palsy, Lethagrie,
> The quartan Ague, dropsy, Lunacy."

The third quaternion is a dialogue between the four seasons, each of which sings her own praises. Spring tells of her months,— March, April, May. In May,—

> "The Sun now enters loving *Gemini*,
> And heats us with the glances of his eye.
> Our thicker raiment makes us lay aside
> Lest by his fervor we be torrifi'd.

> Now swarms the busy, witty, honey-Bee,
> Whose praise deserves a page from more than me
> The cleanly Huswifes Dary's now in th' prime,
> Her shelves and firkins fill'd for winter time."

Summer appears, "Wiping the sweat from off her face that ran," and recounts her treasures. Autumn brings her vintage: —

> "Beaf, Brawn, and Pork are now in great request,
> And solid meats our stomacks can digest.
> This time warm cloaths, full diet and good fires,
> Our pinched flesh, and hungry mawes requires:
> Old, cold, dry Age, and Earth *Autumn* resembles,
> And Melancholy which most of all dissembles.
>
> . . . . . .
>
> "Cold, moist, young flegmy winter now doth lye
> In swadling Clouts, like new born Infancy.
>
> . . . . . .
>
> "Cold frozen *January* next comes in,
> Chilling the blood and shrinking up the skin;
> The day much longer than it was before,
> The cold not lessened, but augmented more.
> Now Toes and Ears, and Fingers often freeze,
> And Travelers their noses sometimes leese."

The poem on "The Four Monarchies" is simply a rhymed version of Raleigh's "History of the World." Tedious reading it would prove now, but in its day it was received with enthusiasm. This was useful poetry, with nothing trivial or frivolous about it, — no poetic fiction either, but good hard facts. In the poem about Queen Elizabeth Mrs. Bradstreet once more takes up the cudgels in defence of women: —

> "She hath wip'd off th' aspersion of her Sex
> That women wisdome lack to play the Rex.
> . . . . . .
> Now say, have women worth? or have they none?
> Or had they some, but with our queen is 't gone?
> Nay Masculines, you have thus tax'd us long;
> But she, though dead, will vindicate our wrong.
> Let such as say our Sex is void of Reason,
> Know tis Slander now but once was Treason."

When Anne Bradstreet died, great was the mourning all over New England. Sermons were preached in all the churches, and funeral elegies by the score poured in upon the family. A few lines from the one written by the Rev. John Norton may serve as a sample of the manner and method of all: —

"A Funeral Elogy, upon that Pattern and Patron of Virtue, the truly pious, peerless and matchless Gentlewoman

   Mrs. Anne Bradstreet, right Panaretes,
Mirror of her Age, Glory of her Sex, whose Heaven-born-Soul leaving its earthly Shrine, chose its native home, and was taken to its Rest, upon the 16th Sept. 1672.

> "Ask not why hearts turn Magazines of passions,
> And why that grief is clad in sev'ral fashions.
> Ask not why some in mournfull black are clad;
> The Sun is set, there needs must be a shade.
> Some do for anguish weep, for anger I
> That Ignorance should live, and Art should die.
> Black, fatal, dismal, inauspicious day,
> Unblest forever by Sol's precious Ray," etc., etc.

There are four hundred pages of Anne Bradstreet's poems; and though a great deal of it is rubbish, there is, now and then, an ingot which shows that she had really the poetic endowment. We can but regret that instead of singing the elements and the ancient monarchies, she did not turn the attention of her muse to the life about her, to the strange new experience through which she was passing, and to the feelings that stirred within her own heart. What would we not give for a woman's view of those days?

Next to Anne Bradstreet in our colonial literature comes a name which was, for more than a hundred years, a household word in New England, — the name of Michael Wigglesworth, whom we must consider as the Puritan Dante, or rather the New England Dante. If Taine called "Paradise Lost" the "epic of damnation and grace" what would he say of Wigglesworth's "Day of Doom"? He might truly call it the doggerel of "damnation and grace." And yet the man had no thought of producing anything humorous or amusing. He was as sadly in earnest in warning his generation as was Dante himself when he made his pilgrimage through the three worlds of the dead. Wigglesworth was the faithful and beloved pastor of the church at Malden for over fifty years. And, although himself a "frail feeble shadow of a man," as Cotton Mather calls him, he was at the same time their physician, healing the body as well as the soul. When ill health compelled him, for a while, to lay aside his work, he employed his time in an attempt to embody his teachings in poetic form, in order to reach a wider audience. The result was that remarkable book, the "Day of Doom."

In order properly to estimate this singular book, we must endeavor to place ourselves, for a time, in the atmosphere in which it was created. We must go back two hundred years and picture to ourselves the weak community, not a nation, not even a state, but a few small detached villages, always in danger from the Indians, and relying constantly on the Lord for protection. They believed themselves the chosen people of God, as much as ever the Israelites did, trying to govern their little body according to God's will, basing their laws on the Old Testament and giving a text for every law. They were made more rigid and more careful in their life by the reports which continually reached them of the gross immorality that was rife in England during the reign of the Merry Monarch, Charles II. At every fresh scandal, the Puritan drew his creed more tightly about him and watched more jealously over those entrusted to his care. And, stern though it seems to us, the sentence which condemned Hester Prynne to stand in the market-place and to wear the "Scarlet Letter" as a warning to other women, was kindness itself compared to the cruelty of the sentiment prevailing in London, that every woman was the natural prey of the man who looked upon her. To understand the high ideal of the Puritans we have only to compare the diary of Judge Sewall with that of Pepys, both written at the same time. The one inspired by "plain living and high thinking," the other by high living and no thinking. Mindful of all the sin and danger there was in the world, the Puritan's aim was not to make the world happy, but to get safely through it and into the next one. Colman's words on Cotton Mather were true of almost every one. "Of death and eternity he was ever speaking with pleasure and desire." It is to be remembered that theology and argument were their daily food and that they were firm in the faith that their belief was the only safe one. It is sad to read that even this chosen community, which made it the object of life to keep in the right way, was beset with " 82 pestilent heresies." When we remember all these things and try to surround ourselves with that atmosphere of the olden time, we can understand that Michael Wigglesworth meant his "Day of Doom" not as a sulphurous denunciation of the wicked, but as a solemn warning to those for whom he was responsible.

The poem is called "The Day of Doom; or a Poetical Description of the Great and Last Judgement." It opens with a picture of the heedlessness and indifference of the world just before the Judgment.

> "Still was the night, serene and bright,
>   When all Men sleeping lay;
> Calm was the Season, and carnal Reason
>   thought so 'twould last for aye.
>
> "4 They put away the evil day,
>   and drown'd their cares and fears,
> Till drown'd were they, and swept away
>   by vengeance unawares;
> So at the last, while men sleep fast
>   in their security,
> Surpris'd they are in such a snare
>   as cometh suddenly."

The Day of Doom suddenly bursts upon this sleeping world.

> "5 For at midnight break forth a Light,
>   which turn'd the night to day,
> And speedily an hideous cry
>   did all the world dismay.

> Sinners awake, their hearts do ake,
>   trembling their loines surprizeth;
> Amaz'd with fear, by what they hear,
>   each one of them ariseth.
>
> "6 They rush from Beds with giddy heads,
>   and to their windows run,
> Viewing this light, which shines more bright
>   than doth the Noon-day Sun."

Christ, the Judge, appears with his train.

> "10 No heart so bold, but now grows cold
>   and almost dead with fear:
> No eye so dry, but now can cry,
>   and pour out many a tear."

In their terror some hide themselves in caves, some leap into the sea, and others flee to the mountains to escape the dread presence. The mountains smoke, the sea roars, the earth is rent and torn. The trump is sounded; the dead arise from their graves, the living are brought out of their hiding places, and all are taken before the judgment seat. The sheep are separated from the goats and placed at His right hand.

" 27 At Christ's left hand the Goats do stand,
all whining hypocrites,
Who for self-ends did seem Christ's friends,
but foster'd guileful sprites :

" 28 Apostates base, and Run-aways,
such as have Christ forsaken,
Of whom the Devil, with seven more evil,
hath fresh possession taken :

" 31 Blasphemers lewd, and swearers shrewd,
Scoffers at purity,
That hated God, contemn'd his Rod,
and lov'd Security.
Sabbath polluters, Saints persecutors,
presumptuous men and proud,
Who never lov'd those that reprov'd
all stand amongst this Crowd.

" 33 False-witness-bearers, and self-forswearers
Murd'rers and Men of blood,
Witches, Inchanters, and Ale-house-haunters,
beyond account there stood.

" 34 There stands all Nations and Generations
of Adam's Progeny,
Whom Christ redeem'd not, who Christ
esteem'd not,
through Infidelity.

> "35 These num'rous bands wringing their hands
> and weeping all stand there,
> Filled with anguish, whose hearts do languish
> with self-tormenting fear."

Christ then begins to judge. He speaks first to the sheep, explaining how and why they are saved, and points them to thrones near by where they are to assist in judging the rest. Then comes the turn of the wicked.

> "51 Of wicked Men, none are so mean
> as there to be neglected :
> Nor none so high in dignity,
> as there to be respected."

Different classes of sins are judged in their order. First hypocrites are disposed of, then "civil honest men," those that pretend want of opportunity to repent, heathen men, and so on, until at last come the reprobate infants.

> "166 Then to the Bar, all they drew near
> who dy'd in infancy,
> And never had or good or bad
> effected pers'nally.

> But from the womb unto the tomb
> were straightway carried,
> (Or, at the least, e're they transgrest)
> who thus began to plead."

The children argue that they should not be punished for Adam's sin, but the Judge replies promptly that they themselves are sinners and must expect to be treated as such.

> "180 Yet to compare your sin with their
> who liv'd a longer time,
> I do confess yours is much less,
> though every sin 's a crime.
>
> "181 A Crime it is, therefore in bliss
> you may not hope to dwell?
> But unto you I shall allow
> the easiest room in Hell."

The pleading is all ended, the earth's foundation is fired, and the sentence of doom pronounced.

> "201 Ye sinful wights, and cursed sprites,
> that work iniquity
> Depart together from me forever
> to endless Misery;

"212 But who can tell the plagues of Hell,
   and torments exquisite?
 Who can relate their dismal state,
   and terrours infinite?

"214 But, ah the wo they undergo
   (they more than all besides)
 Who had the light, and knew the right,
   yet would not it abide.
 The sev'n fold smart, which to their part,
   and portion doth fall,
 Who Christ his Grace would not embrace,
   nor harken to his call.

"211 They live to lie in misery,
   and bear eternal wo;
 And live they must whilst God is just,
   that he may plague them so."

And there the author leaves them while he returns to celebrate the felicity of the saints, who are not at all disturbed by the sufferings of their relatives and friends below. We are frankly told that "they're not dejected nor aught affected with all their misery." All natural affections seem to be done away with. The mother disowns her children who are not saved; and the pious father delights to see his son "In Hell with Devils, for all his evils, burning eternally." It is true that sympathy formerly moved them to wish to share the woes of others, but now, he says, "such compassion is out of fashion, and wholly laid aside."

> "197 One natural Brother beholds another
> in his astonied fit,
> Yet sorrows not thereat a jot,
> nor pities him a whit.
> The godly wife conceives no grief,
> nor can she shed a tear,
> For the sad fate of her dear Mate,
> when she his doom doth hear.

> "198 He that was erst a Husband pierc'd
> with sense of wives distress,
> Whose tender heart did bear the part
> of all her grievances,
> Shall mourn no more as heretofore,
> because of her ill plight;
> Although he see her now to be
> a damn'd forsaken wight."

The swinging sing-song ballad style in which it was written added much to the popularity of the poem. No other book ever published in America has had so large a circulation in proportion to the population of the country, as did the "Day of Doom." Eighteen hundred copies were sold the first year, so that at least every fifth family owned a copy. It was the solace, says Lowell, of every fireside. Children learned it by heart, down to the time of the Revolution. For more than a hundred years it was the representative poem of New England, and Cotton Mather predicted that it would continue to be read in New England until the day of doom itself should arrive.

Toleration is a broad thing. It was George Eliot who pointed out that to be truly liberal you must learn to tolerate intolerance. We can at least try to understand its motives. Instead of scoffing at the narrowness and bigotry of the Puritan we can endeavor to judge him by the standard of the seventeenth century and not that of the nineteenth century. We shall find that instead of being narrower than his generation he was, in all essentials, broader. If he drove out a heretic now and then, it was because, in their hand-to-hand battle for existence, he did not dare to run the risk of the presence of a disturbing element. Those were dark days for Protestantism, and men needed to be on their guard. The fires of the inquisition were still smoking in Spain; Holland had been well-nigh blotted from the face of the earth; Germany had been for thirty years a bloody battle-field, and France had driven the whole of her thinking population into exile. In England the dungeons were overflowing with men whose only crime was attending a dissenting church, and the horrors of torture inflicted on the Scotch Presbyterians make the blood run cold at the recital. What wonder that the second generation of Puritans were more strict than the first? As for superstition, — if the Puritans believed in witches, how was it with the rest of the world? There was not a nation in Europe in which a belief in demoniacal possession was not prevalent. For every witch hung in Boston or Salem thousands were put to death in England, in Germany, Switzerland, and Italy. Nor was theology the only science which was still groping in darkness. Other sciences were yet in the grasp of superstition, notably the science of medicine. Witness the following prescription, sent by Sir Kenelm Digby, a London physician, to John Winthrop, Jr. "For all sorts of agues, I have of late tried the following magnetical experiment with infallible success. Pare the patient's nails when the fit is coming on, and put the parings into a little bag of fine linen or sarsanet, and tie that about a live eel's neck in a tub of water. The eel will die and the patient will recover. And if a dog or a hog eat that eel, they will also die."

In short, looking the world over in the seventeenth century we find that the New

England Puritan compares very favorably with other men. He may have been hard and angular, but he was honest, manly, and heroic. What he lacked in art he made up in character, and earnestness is still one of the primal qualities of character. It was not so much an excess of earnestness which we regret, as the direction sometimes taken for its expression. "Were they too earnest," asks Lowell, "in the strife to save their souls alive? That is still the problem which every wise and brave man is life-long in solving. If the Devil takes a less hateful shape to us than to our fathers, he is as busy with us as with them; and if we cannot find it in our hearts to break with a gentleman of so much worldly wisdom, who gives such admirable dinners, and whose manners are so perfect, so much the worse for us." Before we unite too heartily in their condemnation it were better to weigh carefully the words of one who was certainly our equal in liberality. "Next to the fugitives whom Moses led out of Egypt, the little ship-load of outcasts who landed at Plymouth two centuries and a half ago are destined to influence the future of the world. The spiritual thirst of mankind has for ages been quenched at Hebrew fountains; but the embodiment in human institutions of truths uttered by the Son of Man eighteen centuries ago was to be mainly the work of Puritan thought and Puritan self-devotion." *

* James Russell Lowell, in "New England Two Centuries Ago."

INDEX.

INDEX.

ADAMS, JOHN QUINCY, quoted, 48.
Alden, John, 80, 83.
Alden, Captain John, 222.
Alden, Priscilla, 79, 80.
Allerton, Mr., 82.
Amsterdam, 25, 37.
Andros, Sir Edmund, 115, 116, 146.
"Anne," the, 77, 79, 80.

BANCROFT, 16.
Banister, Mr. Thomas, Jr., 159.
Barry, Mr., 15.
Barstow, Goody, 97.
Baxter, Richard, 190.
Bay Psalm Book, 242, *et seq.*
Bellamy, Mr., 91.
Billington, John, 50, 62.
"Body of Liberties," 90, 94.
Bradford, Governor William; first history of the "Old Colony," 11; MS. found, 15; early life of, 17; quoted, 20, 21, 23; life in Holland, 25; quoted, 36, 37, 39, 42–45, 58–60, 65, 74; death of wife, 54; chosen governor, 68; married to Alice Southworth, 79; re-election as governor, 83; writings of, 84; chosen governor for thirtieth time, 85; death, 86.
"Bradford's History," 12, 15, 17.

"Bradford's Letter Book, 12, 13, 14.
Bradford, John, 15.
Bradford, Samuel, 15.
Bradstreet, Anne, 249, *et seq.*
Bradstreet, Dudley, 222.
Bradstreet, Governor Simon, 197.
Brewster, William, aids "Separatists," 18, 19; imprisoned, 22; made assistant pastor, 26; accompanies Pilgrims, 34; cares for the sick, 60, 72, 80; moves to Duxbury, 84.
Browne, Sir Thomas, 190.
Bryant, Mr., 97.
Burial Hill, 86.
Burroughs, Rev. Mr., 208.
Buxton, Dr. Samuel, 156.

CALEF, ROBERT, 226.
Cape Cod, 42, 45, 48, 50.
Carver, John, elected governor, 49, 58; Received Massasoit, 63; death, 67.
Carpenter, Mary, 171.
Charles II., 115, 131, 135, 144, 261.
Chester, Bishop of, 191.
Clark, Mr. James, 14.
Clark, Mr. Timothy, 174.
Clark's Island, 52.
Clifton, Pastor, 19.

INDEX.

Cloyse, Sarah, 208.
Copp's Hill, 114.
Corey, Giles, 213, 214, 216, 219.
Corey, Martha, 207, 213, 215, 216.
Corwin, Jonathan, 204.
Cotton, Rev. John, 90, 93, 104, 118, 244.
Cushman, Robert, 13.

"DAY OF DOOM," 259-270.
Delft haven, 36, 45.
Denison, Widow, 171, 175.
Digby, Sir Kenelm, 272.
Duxbury, 84.

ELIOT, Rev. ANDREW, 157.
Eliot, Rev. John, 110.
Endicott, Governor, 197.
Everett, Parson, 106.

"FATHER OF AMERICAN HISTORY," the, 11.
Fiske, John, quoted, 187.
"Fortune," the, 72.
Freneau, Phillip, 235.

GALLOWS HILL, 213, 223.
Gibbs, Mrs. Mary, 179, 180.
Glover, Goody, 193.
Good, Sarah, 203-206.
Goodman, John, 57.
Griggs, Dr., 201.

HALE, Mrs., 225.
Hale, Rev. Mr., 225.
Hathorne, John, 204.
Hely, Goodman, 102.
Hibbins, Ann, 197.
Higginson, Rev. Francis, 92.
Higginson, Thomas Wentworth, quoted, 105, 113.

Hobbs, Deliverance, 222.
Hooker, Thomas, 113.
Hopkins, Matthew, 192.
Hopkins, Oceanus, 41.
Hubbard, Elizabeth, 211, 212.
Hull, Hannah, 137.
Hutchinson, Ann, 188.

JAMES II., 115, 116, 146.
Johnson's "Wonder Working Providence," 92.
Jones, Margaret, 197.

LAUD, ARCHBISHOP, 16, 113.
Lawson, Rev. Mr., 201, 207.
Lechford, Thomas, 95.
Leyden, 13, 25, 29, 34.
Lidget, Captain, 133.
"Little James," the, 77.
Lowell, James Russell, quoted, 229, 270, 273.
Lyford, Mr., 81.

MACAULAY, quoted, 235.
"Magnalia Christi Americana," 110, 124.
Massachusetts Historical Society, 13, 16, 134.
Massasoit, 63, 65, 71, 77.
Mather, Cotton, 84; quoted, 110; tomb, 114, 118; youth, 119; called to the North Church, 120; belief in witchcraft, 122, 123; writings, 124; sermon, 140, 146; quarrel with Sewall, 166; sermon in defence of periwigs, 169, 189, 262, 270.
Mather, Increase, sermon, 109; prayer for death of King Phillip, 110; diary, 114; sent to England, 116; chooses the

INDEX.

governor, 118; speech on the charter, 144, 146, 166, 209.
Maule, Thomas, 93.
"Mayflower," the, 17, 35; starts on voyage, 38, 39; starts for the third time, 46; compact signed in, 47; anchored at Provincetown, 49, 50; anchored at Plymouth, 54; sent back to England, 66, 67.
Mayhew, 110.
Merrymount, 81.
More, Doctor, 190.
Morton, 14.
Moody, Rev. Joshua, 105.
"Mourt's Relation," 12, 13.

NAUMKEAG, 83.
New Haven Code of Laws, 97.
North Church, 114.
Norton, Rev. John, 257.
Noyes, Rev. Mr., 223.

OLD COLONY, 11.
Oldham, John, 81.
Old South Church, 14, 138, 144, 145.
Oliver, Mistress, 91.
Oliver, Mr., 174.
Osborne, Sarah, 203, 205, 206.

PARKER, THEODORE, 171.
Parris, Rev. Mr., 200, 202, 207, 230.
Parris, Elizabeth, 200.
Pawtucket, 62.
Pemberton, Rev. Mr., 166.
Pepys, 129, 131, 132, 261.
Phelps, Nicholas, 98.
Phipps, Sir William, 118, 148, 209, 222, 224, 227.
Phipps, Lady, 222.

Pilgrims, 12, 13, 16, 26; decided to leave Holland, 34; embarkation, 38; sign compact, 46; landing, 53; begin to build town, 55–57, 66, 67; first duel, 69; famine, 72, 86.
"Phenomena Quædam Apocalyptica," 163.
"Plain Dealing," 95.
Plymouth Rock, 9.
Pomeroy, Jesse, 199.
Prince, Rev. Thomas, 14, 15, 17.
Prince, Governor Thomas, 83.
Plymouth, 10, 12, 15, 17, 274.
Plymouth, England, 39, 45.
Provincetown, 49.
Prynne, Hester, 261.
Prynne, Puritan, 240.
Puritan preacher, 90, 92.
Puritans, popular idea of, 235; character of, 270–274.

QUAKERS, 111, 112, 188.

ROBINSON, Rev. JOHN, 19, 26, 34, 80.
Ruggles, Widow, 179.

SAINT SIMON, diary of, 129, 130, 133.
Samoset, 62, 63.
Sargeant, Thomas, student, 101.
Scott, Thomas, 99.
Scrooby, 18, 19, 22.
"Selling of Joseph," the, 162.
"Separatists," 11, 19, 189.
Sewall, Henry, 134.
Sewall, Betty, 139, 141.
Sewall, Joseph, 139, 174.
Sewall, Mrs., 158, 171.
Sewall, Sam, 142, 148.

Sewall, Judge Samuel, 100, 103, 129; diary, 133; early life, 135; marriage, 137; diary, 137–183; public offices, 143; journey to London, 146; engaged in witchcraft trials, 148; repentance and confession, 149–151; prayer on fast-day, 152–155; duties as judge, 158; writings, 162; opinion on periwigs, 167–170; courtships, 171–180; second marriage, 174; third marriage, 181; character, 182, 183; quoted, 245, 247, 248, 261.
Shephard, Rev. Mr., 113.
Shrimpton, Mr., 133.
Smith, Capt. John, 54, 64.
Southworth, Mistress Alice, 79.
Southampton, 35, 38.
"Speedwell," the, 35, 38–41.
Squanto, 63, 64, 70.
Standish, Barbara, 79.
Standish, Miles, 12; joins the Pilgrims, 35; leads exploring party, 49; cares for the sick, 60, 61; meets Massasoit, 63; ends war with Indians, 77; moves to Duxbury, 83, 85; death, 86.
Standish, Rose, 61.
Stoughton, Lieutenant Governor, 209, 225.

"Talithi Cumi," 162.
Tilly, Mrs. Elizabeth, 173–175.
Tisquantum, 63, 64, 70.
Tituba, 200, 203, 205, 206, 228.
Tomlin, Mr., of Lynn, 101.

Ward, Rev. Nathaniel, 90; quoted, 108, 252.
Wetherell, Parson, 97.
White, Peregrine, 50.
Wigglesworth, Rev. Michael, 106, 259–262.
Williams, Abigail, 200, 201, 212.
Williams, Roger, 113, 188.
Willard, Josiah, 168.
Willard, Rev. Mr., 146.
Winslow, Edward, 11, 34, 80.
Winthrop, Governor, 197, 237.
Winthrop, Madam Katherine, 171, 175, 178, 179.

www.ingramcontent.com/pod-product-compliance
Lightning Source LLC
Chambersburg PA
CBHW031938230426
43672CB00010B/1967